IMMERSION
Bible Studies

APOCRYPHA

In honor of my father,
J. Arthur F. de Silva,
on his eightieth birthday

Praise for IMMERSION

"IMMERSION BIBLE STUDIES is a godsend for participants who desire sound Bible study yet feel they do not have large amounts of time for study and preparation. IMMERSION is concise. It is brief but covers the material well and leads participants to apply the Bible to life. IMMERSION is a wonderful resource for today's church."

Larry R. Baird, senior pastor of Trinity Grand Island United Methodist Church

"If you're looking for a deeper knowledge and understanding of God's Word, you must dive into IMMERSION BIBLE STUDIES. Whether in a group setting or as an individual, you will experience God and his unconditional love for each of us in a whole new way."

Pete Wilson, founding and senior pastor of Cross Point Church

"This beautiful series helps readers become fluent in the words and thoughts of God, for purposes of illumination, strength building, and developing a closer walk with the One who loves us so."

Laurie Beth Jones, author of *Jesus, CEO* and *The Path*

"I highly commend to you IMMERSION BIBLE STUDIES, which tells us what the Bible teaches and how to apply it personally."

John Ed Mathison, author of *Treasures of the Transformed Life*

"The IMMERSION BIBLE STUDIES series is no less than a game changer. It ignites the purpose and power of Scripture by showing us how to do more than just know God or love God; it gives us the tools to love like God as well."

Shane Stanford, author of *You Can't Do Everything . . . So Do Something*

IMMERSION
Bible Studies
APOCRYPHA

David A. deSilva

Abingdon Press

Nashville

APOCRYPHA
IMMERSION BIBLE STUDIES
by David A. deSilva

Library of Congress Cataloging-in-Publication Data

DeSilva, David Arthur.
  Apocrypha / David A. deSilva.
    pages cm. — (Immersion Bible studies)
  ISBN 978-1-4267-4297-2 (unsewn/adhesive bound : alk. paper) 1. Apocryphal books (Old Testament)—Textbooks. I. Title.
BS1700.D428 2013
229'.06—dc23

2013026901

Editor: Marvin W. Cropsey
Leader Guide Writer: Marvin W. Cropsey

13 14 15 16 17 18 19 20 21 22—10 9 8 7 6 5 4 3 2 1

Manufactured in the United States of America

Contents

Review Team

IMMERSION BIBLE STUDIES

A fresh new look at the Bible, from beginning to end,
and what it means in your life.

Welcome to IMMERSION!

We've asked some of the leading Bible scholars, teachers, and pastors to help us with a new kind of Bible study. IMMERSION remains true to Scripture but always asks, "Where are you in your life? What do you struggle with? What makes you rejoice?" Then it helps you read the Scriptures to discover their deep, abiding truths. IMMERSION is about God and God's Word, and it is also about you—not just your thoughts, but your feelings and your faith.

In each study you will prayerfully read the Scripture and reflect on it. Then you will engage it in three ways:

Claim Your Story
> Through stories and questions, think about your life, with its struggles and joys.

Enter the Bible Story
> Explore Scripture and consider what God is saying to you.

Live the Story
> Reflect on what you have discovered, and put it into practice in your life.

IMMERSION makes use of an exciting new translation of Scripture, the Common English Bible (CEB). The CEB and IMMERSION BIBLE STUDIES will offer adults:

- the emotional expectation to find the love of God
- the rational expectation to find the knowledge of God
- reliable, genuine, and credible power to transform lives
- clarity of language

Whether you are using the Common English Bible or another translation, IMMERSION BIBLE STUDIES will offer a refreshing plunge into God's Word, your life, and your life with God.

1.

What Is the Apocrypha, and Why Should We Care?

Apocrypha

Claim Your Story

I was raised in the Episcopal Church, and my first encounters with the Apocrypha were positive ones. Serving as an acolyte at weddings and funerals, I heard readings from Tobit and the Wisdom of Solomon during these special services. Every now and again, a selection from Sirach or Baruch would be read on a Sunday morning as part of the lectionary cycle. It struck me as a little odd that these books were not in the pew Bibles, nor in any of our Bibles at home. On the other hand, they sure sounded *scriptural*. When I was a teenager, I found a copy of the Apocrypha in the church library, began to acquaint myself better with the whole collection, and came to appreciate and highly value each book's witness.

The experience of many of my friends and students, however, was quite different. Some of them assert that good Christians shouldn't even *read* the Apocrypha. "These books are theologically suspect," they say. "They were purposefully excluded from the Bible. They are what Catholics read." The Apocrypha can be a tough sell in many Protestant Christian circles. It was not self-evident that there should even be an IMMERSION BIBLE STUDIES volume on the Apocrypha, since these books are not part of the Bible for the majority of those who will use this series.

What experiences have you had with the Apocrypha up to this point? What are your own impressions of it as you begin this study? What do you hope to discover as a result of participating in this study?

Enter the Bible Story

The Apocrypha is a collection of Jewish texts written between about 250 B.C. and A.D. 100, offering what has been well called a "bridge between the Testaments" (though a few texts overlap with the writing of the New Testament). These books are essential reading if, for no other reason, than to fill in gaps in our knowledge of the Jewish matrix into which Jesus was born and within which the movement in his name took shape.

The Apocrypha: An Overview

Book	Summary	Origins	Significance
Tobit	A fictional story about God's deliverance of two faithful families from distress.	Palestine or Eastern Mediterranean, in Hebrew or Aramaic, between 250 and 100 B.C.	Insights into Jewish ethics, beliefs about divine intervention, and hopes for the nation's future during the intertestamental period.
Judith	A fictional story about God's deliverance of a besieged city and the entire nation through the actions of a brave woman.	Judea, in Hebrew, probably between 142 and 63 B.C.	Affirmation of the validity of Deuteronomy's theology of the covenant and the nation's fortunes, and of God's ability to bring victory to the weaker power.
Esther (Greek)	An expanded version of the Hebrew Esther, making God's activity and the piety of its main characters explicit.	Some additions originate in Judea, in Hebrew, before 100 B.C. Others originate in the Western Diaspora, in Greek (perhaps Egypt).	Insights into causes of Jew-Gentile tensions, windows into personal piety; instance of "rewriting" Scripture.
Wisdom of Solomon	An essay on the importance of living with eternity in view, the nature of Wisdom, and God's justice and providence as revealed in the Exodus story.	The Egyptian Jewish community (perhaps Alexandria), in Greek, between 50 B.C. and A.D. 30.	Contributions to ethics (connecting view of afterlife with ethical practice), criticism of Gentile religion, and theological developments (persona of Wisdom).

Book	Summary	Origins	Significance
Sirach	A sizable collection of the curriculum taught in one sage's wisdom school, ranging from theological topics to ethics to domestic, social, and political advice.	Jerusalem, in Hebrew, between 200 and 175 B.C.	Opens windows into every corner of (elite) Jewish life; avidly promoted Torah observance in a time of accommodation to Greek practice.
Baruch	An anthology of material relevant to life under Gentile domination, including a national prayer of confession and repentance, a wisdom poem commending Torah observance, and prophetic material consoling Jerusalem and predicting restoration.	Palestine or Eastern Diaspora, in Hebrew (save for 5:5-9, added in Greek), probably between 164 and 100 B.C.	Highlights what parts of the scriptural tradition were especially relevant to Jews experiencing foreign rule, drawing them together into a "program" for restoration.
Letter of Jeremiah	A short tract urging Jews living in Gentile territories not to be moved by the Gentiles' displays of piety to think that there is something to their idolatrous religions.	Palestine or Eastern Diaspora, in Hebrew, between 317 and 100 B.C.	Example of the need for, and manner of, insulating Jews from the opinion and practice of the Gentile majority.
Additions to Daniel	Two additional tales involving Daniel (Susanna, Bel and the Snake) and two psalms inserted into Daniel 3 (Prayer of Azariah, a psalm of repentance, and Hymn of the Three Young Men, a psalm of praise).	Probably Palestine, in Hebrew, prior to 100 B.C.	Windows into issues *within* the Jewish community, critique of Gentile religion, and personal piety (particularly the crafting of new prayers and psalms).
First Maccabees	A history of the Hellenizing Reform and Maccabean Revolution from 168 to 141 B.C.	Judea, in Hebrew, sometime after 140 B.C.	An essential historical source, told with a view to promoting the Hasmonean dynasty.

APOCRYPHA

Book	Summary	Origins	Significance
Second Maccabees	A history of the Hellenizing Reform and Maccabean Revolution from 175 to 161 B.C.	Judea or Western Diaspora, in Greek, sometime before 124 B.C.	An essential historical source, told with a view to promoting Torah observance.
First Esdras	An alternative version of the story found in 2 Chronicles 35–36; Ezra; Nehemiah 8.	Western Diaspora, in Greek, between 200 B.C. and A.D. 50.	Contains an additional story ("the contest of the three bodyguards") elevating Zerubbabel.
Prayer of Manasseh	A prayer of confession and repentance attributed to Manasseh (see 2 Chronicles 33:18-19).	Diaspora origin, probably in Greek, between 250 B.C. and A.D. 50.	Expression of personal piety and the view of God as deeply compassionate and forgiving.
Psalm 151	A blending of two originally separate psalms celebrating David's selection by Samuel and David's defeat of Goliath.	The original psalms were written in Palestine, in Hebrew, between the fourth and first centuries B.C.	Witness to the ongoing liturgical creativity of Jewish poets.
Third Maccabees	A work of historical fiction telling of the persecution of Jews in Egypt and their miraculous deliverance.	Egyptian Jewish community, in Greek, probably between 31 B.C. and A.D. 41.	Window into Jew-Gentile tensions and their causes, especially social and political issues.
Second Esdras	A Jewish apocalypse dealing with questions of God's justice in the aftermath of Jerusalem's destruction in A.D. 70	Judea or surrounding area, in Hebrew, about A.D. 100.	An honest attempt to wrestle with serious theological issues in the form of an apocalypse.
Fourth Maccabees	A philosophical speech about following the Jewish Torah as the best way to learn to master emotions, desires, and sensations with a view to living virtuously.	Jewish communities in Southern Turkey, in Greek, between A.D. 25 and 100.	A window into the use of Greek ethical philosophy in the service of interpreting and promoting the Jewish way of life.

There are really two stories to enter in order to orient ourselves to this collection. The first is the story of the Jewish people from Alexander the Great's conquest of in 332 B.C. through Rome's suppression of the Jewish Revolt of A.D. 66–70. The books of the Apocrypha emerge as a response to the challenges Jews face as this story of foreign domination progresses. The second is the story of how these particular Jewish texts came to be differentiated from the vast amount of Jewish literature written during this period, and thus became a collection that can be defined as "the Apocrypha." This would be the story of the value placed on these particular books by Christians throughout the ages.

The World Behind the Apocrypha

The story told in the Hebrew Bible (Old Testament) takes readers up to the Persian period, with Cyrus of Persia conquering Babylon and authorizing the return of uprooted, conquered peoples to their homelands. Cyrus thus becomes a hero for the Jewish people, allowing the exiles of Judah to return to rebuild its Temple (completed by 515 B.C.) and Jerusalem with its city walls (completed after 445 B.C.). The next events found in the Protestant Bible concern the last years of King Herod of Judea, who died in 4 B.C.!

A lot happened in between, much of this the direct or indirect result of the exploits of Alexander the Great. Alexander seized all of the Persian Empire's western lands, including Judah, by 331 B.C. By the time of his death in 323, he had expanded his Greek empire east past Babylon itself. Alexander's generals divided his empire between them in the decades following his death. The descendants of General Ptolemy ruled Egypt as their empire; the descendants of General Seleucus ruled Syria, Babylonia, and part of Asia Minor as theirs. Palestine was the disputed buffer zone, held by the Ptolemies of Egypt until Antiochus III decisively secured it for the Seleucid Empire in 198 B.C.

During this period, many elite Jews sought to secure their future through assimilating to the dominant powers to some extent. Many learned Greek. Some took Greek names in order to be identified less with a conquered people. Some adapted more freely to Greek customs and expectations to the point that they no longer looked Jewish at all. In 175 B.C., the high priest himself took the decisive step of re-founding Jerusalem as a Greek city, enrolling like-minded Jews in its senate and setting up the institutions for full-fledged Greek education and acculturation. This led to disastrous consequences: a brutal repression of Judaism and the rededication of the Temple itself to foreign gods. It also gave rise to the Maccabean Revolt, the purification of the Temple (to be celebrated ever after in Hanukkah), and the establishing of an independent Jewish state under the Hasmonean dynasty (read First and Second Maccabees for the details).

Judah enjoyed political independence for about eighty years (141 to 63 B.C.), but the Hasmonean rulers lost both credibility and power, with the result that Rome took Judea under its "protection" and established Herod as its deputy king. Roman rule, first through Herod's family and then directly, was experienced as oppressive and unwelcome, leading to an ill-advised revolt against Rome in A.D. 66–70. The Roman armies crushed the opposition and laid waste to the Temple for a second traumatic time.

Wrestling With Faithfulness in an Age of Domination

The social, cultural, and political dynamics of this period presented many challenges for Jews living in Judea. These challenges were often magnified for Jews living in "Diaspora," that is, in Jewish communities in Egypt, Syria, or other Gentile territories. This was an environment that tended to intensify their experience of living as a minority group in a very un-Jewish world. Many of the books of the Apocrypha can be read as attempts to nurture and discern faithful responses to these challenges, helping Jews to remain connected to the God who spoke in the Scriptures and who continued to be present to guide, sustain, and deliver.

A major challenge had to do with the choice between assimilation and remaining "holy to the Lord," hence keeping cultural and social distance from non-Jews. Does keeping covenant make sense in a multicultural environment dominated by the Greeks? Why keep walking *this* path, especially when it makes networking, fitting in, and prospering *more* challenging? What is the best path to individual and national prosperity?

Sirach, Tobit, Judith, and First through Fourth Maccabees all give prominence to addressing these questions. Greek Esther and Third Maccabees bear witness to close Torah-observance, and Gentile reactions to the Jews' practices, as a source of unwelcome, unhelpful ethnic tension.

Another important challenge comes from the Jews' increasing awareness of their minority status and opinion. They were asking, "do our claims about God's uniqueness make sense in a pluralistic world where the majority worship other gods with just as much fervency?" The Letter of Jeremiah, stories like Bel and the Snake, and the second half of Wisdom of Solomon were written to answer this question.

Living under near-constant foreign domination for centuries posed challenges to belief in the assurances made to David and his line and the visions of Zion's future articulated in the Hebrew Scriptures. Have the promises failed? Tobit and Baruch seek to reaffirm the promises in the context of Greek domination, while Second Esdras raises the problem most acutely in the wake of Rome's destruction of the second Temple. From a different angle, the opening chapters of Wisdom of Solomon and the martyr narratives of Second and Fourth Maccabees raise and answer the question in regard to the individual righteous person who, nevertheless, does not enjoy God's rewards in this life.

The Hellenistic context was not all bad, however. It also provided opportunities for the expansion of Jewish wisdom and cultural knowledge, as well as for the creative reinterpretation of the value of the Jewish way of life. Sirach, Wisdom of Solomon, and Fourth Maccabees especially bear witness to the phenomenon of Hellenism's positive contribution to the repertoire of Jewish wisdom and self-understanding.

Christian Reading Practices and the Apocrypha

Jews wrote a vast amount of literature during this period. The fact that we have a collection called the Apocrypha at all is the result of conversations among Christians about the value and importance of these *particular* books from that much larger body. Early Christians read and valued many Jewish books that were not considered sacred in the synagogue. This should not surprise us, since they were turning more and more to writings like the letters of its apostolic missionaries and the Gospels as they were shaping their distinctive identity and practice. The early church was not living within the bounds of Judaism, including its boundaries on "canon."

Perhaps because they saw the points of similarity between the teachings of Tobit and Ben Sira and Jesus or between Wisdom of Solomon and Paul, or because they found texts like Second and Fourth Maccabees helpful in their own struggles to endure persecution, these books became very influential in the church alongside the books of the Hebrew Bible. Because the early church tended to use the Greek translations and versions of the books, even of the Hebrew Bible, they also inherited the longer versions of Esther and Daniel as well as the additions to Jeremiah's legacy (Baruch and Letter of Jeremiah). The early church thus had, functionally, a broader set of Jewish Scriptures than the synagogue.

Christians also noticed this difference, and frequently raised questions about whether or not the Christian Old Testament should fall more in line with the Jewish Scriptures. Jerome, a Christian scholar who studied for some time in Palestine, was a fourth-century champion of the latter view. He drew a line between the canonical books of the Old Testament (the Hebrew Bible) and the additional books that, while valued by the church for centuries, should not be held to carry the same level of authority. Augustine avidly opposed this distinction due to the authority and impact these additional books had already enjoyed in the church for centuries. His view became the dominant one, ratified by the Third Council of Carthage in A.D. 397. This is reflected indirectly in the fact that our three oldest copies of the complete Christian Bible (three Greek volumes from the fourth and fifth centuries) contain most of the Apocrypha and intersperse these books throughout the Old Testament without distinction.

The Protestant Reformation, of course, brought this issue to the fore once again with its emphasis on "Scripture alone" as the rule for the church. It became vitally important in such an environment to decide exactly what counted as Scripture. Luther was well aware of the historical debates over the status of the additional books. It did not help their cause that certain beliefs and practices that Luther found objectionable, like offering prayers and masses for the dead or the idea of a "treasury of merit" that could be drawn upon by the less meritorious, were defended on the basis of passages in Tobit and Second Maccabees (Tobit 4:7-11; 2 Maccabees 12:43-45). Luther, followed by other reformers, concluded that these books should be gathered up out of the Old Testament and printed as a separate section, thus the Apocrypha came to be.

It is important to realize, however, that even Martin Luther highly valued these books. First of all, he took the trouble to translate them into German along with the canonical books and to print them in his German Bible. He also stated that, "though [the Apocryphal books] are not esteemed like the holy Scriptures, they are still both useful and good to read" (Luther's preface to the Apocrypha). He presented them thus as "recommended reading" alongside the Protestant canon. The Zurich Bible also included the Apocrypha as a separate section, with Ulrich Zwingli (Swiss Reformation leader, 1484–1531) commending them as containing "much that is true and useful, fostering piety of life and edification." They were included also in the original publication of the King James Bible. They were gradually omitted out of an interest in publishing less expensive Bibles for personal use, missionary distribution, and eventually church use.

The existence of the collection of Apocrypha, therefore, is the result of two equal dynamics—the exceptional value that the church placed on these texts and doubts about that value equaling that of the books of the Hebrew canon.

Live the Story

I find the authors of the Apocrypha to be very much kindred spirits to our own. We ask many of the same questions that they did: How do we find guidance from God in a post-scriptural age, that is, when we hold that the golden age of divine inspiration is behind us? How do we remain faithful to the revelation we have received (our Scriptures and their message) in a significantly changed world? How can we recognize the challenges to our faith and faithfulness? How can we positively engage this world in ways that do not corrode, and might even nourish, our faith and faithfulness?

We also share the conviction that, while we might not be living in a period in which inspired Scriptures are being written, God is not truly silent, either. Rather, God is still guiding God's people, inspiring faithful responses and the diligent seeking of God's will and favor. At the very least, we can approach these texts as the devotional and inspirational literature most widely, and for the longest time, embraced by the Christian church throughout the world.

2.

Tobit

Tobit 1–14

Claim Your Story

Many of us will resonate with the plights of Tobit and of Sarah, if not in all the particulars of their stories, at least in the place to which their stories had brought them—the place of being ready to give up because there seems to be no way forward. We lose jobs and the means of sustaining our families and ourselves. We suffer personal injury or lose essential abilities. Our marriages fail to last and to produce the fruit for which we were hoping. Our commitment to doing what is right doesn't seem to pay off. Not all of us, but at least some of us have come to a point at some time in our lives where we've stopped praying "God, help me find a way forward" and found ourselves praying "God, just end my misery."

I've been at that point at least twice so far in my life. Perhaps twice in forty-five years is not all that bad. I resonate with Tobit's and Sarah's stories because, like them by the end of the book, I can look back on such prayers and praise God for making a way forward when there appeared to be none, not even the possibility. The Book of Tobit is a reminder that today's hopeless crisis can become tomorrow's testimony to God's generous kindness.

Enter the Bible Story

King David was remembered as "a man who shares [God's] desires" (Acts 13:22), or, in more traditional language, "a man after [God's] own heart" (1 Samuel 13:14, NRSV). God worked mighty acts through David and on David's behalf. The Psalms bear witness to David's many prayers *and* God's many answers. But David was king over God's people. Of course God took notice of him and invested in him. What about ordinary people, the people about whom the great historical books of the Old Testament say nothing (except, perhaps, that so many were killed in this or that battle, or so many participated in this building project, or so many returned to Judea from this or that tribe)?

The Book of Tobit fills an important gap in this regard. It is the story of an ordinary man, his wife, their son, and their extended family, who find themselves at the ends of their respective ropes, and who pray to God for help. They're not kings; they're not prophets. They're just "good church folk." And it is the story of how God hears their prayers and intervenes to bring about a good outcome beyond anyone's expectations. As such, the book assures us that the God who was close to, and interacted with the stories of, the great people of the Bible is also close to and ready to intervene in the lives of us ordinary folk as well.

About the Text

Some History of Tobit's Book

The Book of Tobit appears to have enjoyed a widespread circulation among Jewish readers. Fragments of five different copies of Tobit (four written in Aramaic, one in Hebrew) were discovered among the Dead Sea Scrolls, the library of the Jewish sect at Qumran. The number of manuscripts of a particular book in such a collection generally reflects the importance of the book for the community (manuscripts of Deuteronomy, Isaiah, and the Psalms each numbered in the twenties in the Qumran caves). The earliest of these manuscripts of Tobit dates from about 100 B.C., showing that the book itself was written at least before that date. The Qumran manuscripts also confirm that the longer of the two Greek versions of Tobit known in the ancient world was probably the more original, hence the privileging of this longer version in the CEB.

Prayer

The Book of Tobit is a well-crafted, delightful story. Unlike many narratives from the ancient world, where the turning point comes rather late in the story just before the resolution, the turning point in Tobit comes quite early and in a rather nondramatic fashion. That turning point is a pair of prayers in Chapter 3.

Tobit, an Israelite exile living in Nineveh, has lost his sight and become entirely dependent on the wages his wife, Anna, is able to earn. When he refuses to believe her employers were so generous as to send a young goat home with her as a bonus, she replies with words that strike him to the heart, recalling his *former* ability to be generous himself. This pushes him over the edge, and he prays that God would at last allow him to die, since life has become so unbearable. At the same time, three hundred miles away in Ecbatana, a young woman named Sarah is similarly distraught. After seven marriages that end on the wedding night, she loses hope of ever having a family. Her female servants have started a rumor that she kills her husbands on their wedding night and spit her bad fortune in her face. On the verge of committing suicide, she decides not to bring even more grief on her family by her own hand and prays to God either to kill her or take notice of her pain at last.

The narrator takes us thence to God's throne and to God's decisive action on behalf of Tobit and Sarah to turn things around for them. The remainder of the story—the vast bulk of the story—is not a journey in search of resolution, but the story of how the resolution of the whole family's ills is being worked out along the way. This is itself quite a statement about life with God. Like the characters in the story, we may not comprehend as it is happening, but in hindsight we can at last see that a greater part of our story is the story of God working out the resolution better than we might have imagined.

The second thing to notice is that God hears prayer and answers in the particular way that God wishes. Neither Tobit's nor Sarah's prayer was equal to God's generosity, and neither could have foreseen that God would do so much more than they could have asked or imagined. Their words asked for death, but God heard the cry of their hearts to see God's goodness toward them in the land of the living. And so Christians have since frequently asked God, as for example in the words of the Book of Common Prayer, to "accept and fulfill our petitions, we pray, not as we ask in our ignorance, nor as we deserve in our sinfulness, but as you know and love us in your Son Jesus Christ our Lord."

Courage

A second theme underlying the Book of Tobit focuses on the need to find the courage to go forward, the courage that comes from believing that God *will* help, that God *will* make a way, that God will *not* add grief upon grief forever.

When Tobit proposes to send their son Tobias on a potentially hazardous journey to distant Rages to recover a good sum of money Tobit had left in deposit there decades before, his wife, Anna, strongly prefers to keep Tobias safe at home. She displays a noble willingness to allow the money deposited in Rages to remain uncollected as a "ransom" for their son's safety. Tobit urges her to trust, even after all the ill that has befallen them, that God will send a good angel with Tobias to keep him safe and allow him to accomplish his mission. We should remember that Tobit is not thinking of himself in regard to recovering this money. He expects God to have heard his prayer for death and is trying to make provision for his son, Tobias, and his wife, Anna, before God answers his prayer, leaving Anna a widow.

We find something similar later in the story when Sarah is about to enter the bridal chamber for the eighth time. Raguel must urge his daughter to move forward in confidence, hoping that God will use this occasion to bring blessing and happiness, despite the fact that seven marriages have ended abruptly and badly. The Book of Tobit challenges the colloquial definition of insanity—doing the same thing over and over again, expecting different results. Because God is in the equation, and because God may always elect to show mercy, the result *could* be different this next time. One must go forward with at least enough faith so that one gives God the chance to intervene beneficently. The fact that Raguel has his servants dig a grave for Tobias—just in case—shows that he is not an unrealistic optimist. But they must brave the possibility of further sorrow and disappointment if they are ever to be surprised by joy.

Being Rich Toward God

Tobit closely followed the commandments laid out in God's Instruction. He didn't offer sacrifices anywhere but Jerusalem (Tobit 1:4-6; 14:5-7; Deuteronomy 12:1-14). He didn't depart from following the food laws even when in Gentile territory (Tobit 1:10-13; Leviticus 11:1-46). But above all else, prior to his own fall into poverty, Tobit was a model for charitable giving and taking care of the less fortunate Jews in his community (Tobit 1:3, 16-18; 2:2-7; Deuteronomy 15:11). Tobit's commitment to showing such love for his neighbor is what gains him notice, according to the author, in God's court (Tobit 12:12-14), resulting in God's commitment to heal Tobit's sight and to bring healing to the larger family through the nonfatal marriage of Tobias and Sarah. The character of Ahikar, known from ancient literature, is brought into the story as Tobit's nephew. He, too, becomes a living model of the benefits of almsgiving not only for those who receive charity, but also for those who give charitably, since God looks to repay the kindnesses of those who give to those who do not have the means to repay a kindness (Tobit 14:10-11).

One of the lessons that Tobit teaches his son Tobias concerns making charitable giving a priority and a regular practice.

> Give aid, my child, according to what you have. If you have a lot, make a donation out of your riches. If you have only a little, don't be afraid to make a donation in proportion. In this way, you will store up a valuable treasure for a time of need. Giving assistance to the poor rescues a person from death and keeps a person from going down into darkness.
>
> (Tobit 4:8-10)

The idea that giving money to those in need is the best way to lay up a treasure for the future will not be new to readers of the Gospels: "Sell your possessions and give to those in need. Make for yourselves wallets that don't wear out—a treasure in heaven that never runs out" (Luke 12:33).

There are many things that money can't buy—a cure for blindness, the exorcism of a demon, safety on a journey, finding the *right* husband or wife. Living in a manner that blesses others and pleases God is, Tobit's story reminds us, the best way to safeguard against life's greater evils.

Hoarding wealth rather than charitable sharing may seem like the best safeguard against an uncertain future, but it would have done nothing for Tobit, Sarah, and their families. Indeed, Tobit *did* accumulate quite a bit of savings during his productive years, but lost access to it all at the most critical time in his life. Our teetering economy has taught many people this same lesson. But the good one has done throughout one's life is a treasure that has lasting value, since God values it and keeps it in God's memory. And, as the author of Hebrews would say much later, "God isn't unjust so that he forgets your efforts and the love you have shown for his name's sake when you served and continue to serve God's holy people" (Hebrews 6:10).

Love and Marriage

I first encountered the Book of Tobit while serving as an acolyte at a wedding in the Episcopal church in which I was raised. The Old Testament lesson was taken from Tobit, one of the suggested readings for weddings in the Book of Common Prayer. The lesson focused on the prayer of Tobias and Sarah on their wedding night (though wisely omitting the part about the love-crazed demon). In this prayer, Tobias looks to the Creation story to identify God's purposes for marriage, one of which was for a person to enjoy a suitable helper along life's journey. Tobias affirms that he is entering into marriage in line with God's good purposes (Tobit 8:6-7). This means, in part, that he and Sarah have chosen each other on the basis of what they understood to be God's criteria for choosing a marriage partner—finding someone similarly committed to God and God's Instruction. The choice was to be from the Israelite people, even from one's own tribe, presumably to preserve the overall inheritance of each tribe in the land of Israel (Tobit 4:12-13). Tobias did not allow other factors (like lust, Tobit 8:7) to lead him astray so as to choose a non-Jewish or otherwise inappropriate life-partner. Rather, the angel's good report of Sarah (her virtues, her lineage and proximity in relationship, her beauty) hits all the right topics to assure Tobias that she would be a good life-partner. And so "he fell deeply in love with her" on this basis, and not on the basis of visual or physical stimulation (Tobit 6:18). Perhaps the most unbelievable aspect of the story, straining credulity more than the medic-inal value of fish guts or the behaviors of amorous demons, is the good relationship we see forged between in-laws on both sides, perhaps a side-effect of the practice of seeking a marriage partner within a network of people who already think highly of one another and feel their larger connections.

The Apocrypha: A Biblical Bridge

Tobit is an excellent example of the bridging nature of the Apocrypha. On the one hand, the story refracts the Old Testament tradition from beginning to end.

Passage from Tobit	Old Testament Background	Connection
Tobit 1:3, 10, 18-21	2 Kings 17:5-18; 18:9-12; 19:35-37	Tobit's story unfolds within the larger story of the Northern Kingdom's fall and Sennacherib's invasion.
Tobit 3:2-5; 14:7	Deuteronomy 28:63-65	Tobit interprets his people's fate in terms of the covenant curses of Deuteronomy.
Tobit 13:2, 5-6; 14:4-7	Deuteronomy 6:5; 30:1-5; 32:39	Tobit affirms that a wide-spread return to covenant loyalty will result in God's restoration of the people.
Tobit 1:4-6; 14:5-7	Deuteronomy 12:1-14; 1 Kings 12:25-33	Tobit rejects the cult site at Bethel, following Deuter-onomy's promotion of the Jerusalem Temple.
Tobit 14:4, 8	Nahum 1:1; 2:13–3:19	Tobit affirms Nahum's pre-diction of Nineveh's fall.
Tobit 13:11; 14:6-7	Isaiah 2:2-3; 60:2-3	The Gentile nations will one day abandon their idols.
Tobit 13:5, 13; 14:7	Isaiah 11:12; 43:5-7; 54:7; Jeremiah 29:13-14	The scattered Jews will one day be gathered together into their ancestral land.
Tobit 13:16; 14:5-6	Isaiah 54:11-12	Jerusalem and its Temple will be restored to their former glory.

Tobit also positively contributes, on the other hand, to the emerging ethics of Jesus' teachings and the movement formed in Jesus' name, as the following table shows.

Passage from Tobit	Passage from the New Testament	Point of comparison
Tobit 4:6b-7	Matthew 5:42; Luke 6:30	One must not turn away empty-handed those who ask for help.
Tobit 4:8-11; 12:8-9	Matthew 6:19-20; 19:21; Luke 12:33-34	Giving one's extra wealth away to those in need now is the way to lay up a reliable treasure against future adversity, rather than stockpiling it to rot.
Tobit 4:15a	Matthew 7:12; Luke 6:31	Tobit is the first Jewish text to give expression to the "Golden Rule." Jesus sharpens the proverb by formulating it positively rather than negatively, using it to urge not only abstaining from harm but also contributing beneficially to others' lives.
Tobit 2:2	Luke 14:12-14	Tobit models exactly the sort of behavior (inviting the poor to one's table) that Jesus would later commend as praiseworthy.
Tobit 14:6-7	Matthew 8:11-12; Luke 13:28-29	Tobit and Jesus share the hope for the conversion of the Gentile nations to the worship of the one God, as well as a tendency to elevate sincerity of love and obedience over ethnic privilege as a requirement of participating in the Kingdom.

Tobias and Sarah's prayer speaks appropriately to both Jewish and Christian couples, calling them to seek their relationships' foundation in their commitment to be good partners for one another above all else, to give each other the consistent, reliable help in matters small and great, spiritual and practical, emotional and physical that is essential to thriving in this life and arriving safely in the harbor of the life to come. Their larger story also challenges us to take more seriously the pronouncement made at weddings that the marriage of two people "unites their families and creates a new one"[1] and to work harder toward the higher ideal of regarding sons- and daughters-in-law as fully one's children as one's natural sons and daughters, and regarding one's spouse's parents as fully one's own second parents as well.

Live the Story

The Book of Tobit challenges us to examine how we are investing our money and other resources. Is your portfolio sufficiently diversified to include laying up treasure against an uncertain future, or as Jesus would put it, "treasure in heaven," by making charitable giving a part of your family budget and sharing your table with the poor a family practice? It often seems to be the case that those who invest themselves more fully in doing what pleases God with their resources have greater confidence that God will also invest in them when their time of need comes. Even Paul, the apostle of "free grace," testifies to the fact that God does care about human beings investing themselves in doing good (Romans 2:7-8). It is not a matter of earning salvation, but it is also not the case that doing good does not matter.

Tobit invites us to honesty in prayer, to throw ourselves before God knowing that God will hear the needs behind the words, the hurts, the desperation. It also tells a story that depicts faith as the courage to keep moving forward even when there seems to be no way, since God might at any time make a way. When you are close to giving up, the author of Tobit would advise you to follow Sarah's example and give it all to God instead, trusting that God will take notice and make a way forward.

1. *The United Methodist Hymnal* (Nashville: The United Methodist Publishing House, 1989), 865.

3.

Second Maccabees

2 Maccabees 2:19–10:38

Claim Your Story

Covenant is a vastly important idea in the Scriptures, so important that the whole of the canon is divided into an Old Covenant and a New Covenant. Jesus announced that God was making a covenant with us, signed and sealed with Jesus' own blood. We are not forced into this covenant agreement. I understand my parents and my church to have spoken for me in infant baptism, declaring that I would be brought up as a member of the covenant people. I voluntarily committed to keep my end of this covenant at my confirmation and many times since while celebrating the renewal of baptismal vows or John Wesley's Service of Covenant Renewal on New Year's Eve. You probably can name a time when you took your place in the covenant people by your own decision.

A covenant is a two-way street: two parties commit to each other and to certain responsibilities. God commits to welcoming us back into God's embrace, taking us into his family, pouring his Holy Spirit into us to empower us to live just and holy lives, and bringing us into a life beyond death. We commit to making the most of God's gifts and letting the Holy Spirit have its way in our lives, taking over as the driving impulse behind all we do.

It's often easy to lose sight, however, of the benefits of persevering in this covenant relationship. We often find ourselves wanting what God has not promised for us—even what God has, in God's good wisdom, no intention of giving us. Do we reach out to get those things for ourselves anyway, even if it means doing what God finds hateful? Or do we continue to place a higher value on God's gifts than on those things that others around us seem to value so highly?

Enter the Bible Story

Scripture is full of warnings about failing to value sufficiently what God has given and wanting something that can only be enjoyed by giving God less than God's due, or by stepping over God's boundaries. Value God's gifts. Don't covet what those who aren't following God might have or enjoy. Don't violate the integrity of your relationship with God in order to get what they might have. This is a constant message in Scripture, and the author of Second Maccabees makes it his theme as he tells the story of what happened in Judea between about 175 and 161 B.C.

The Lessons of Deuteronomy

If the author of Second Maccabees had any goal at all beyond trying to supply an entertaining history of the period, the text suggests that it is to point out that the consequences of keeping the covenant and of breaking the covenant—consequences laid out explicitly and in great detail in Deuteronomy 28–30—are real. And if these consequences are real, as the recent events he recounts demonstrate once again, Jews can do nothing better for themselves and their nation than to pay close attention to God's Instruction, to follow it faithfully day after day.

Deuteronomy is the Greek name for the fifth book of the Old Testament, meaning "a second [statement of the] Law," the formal Instruction God gave to those people whom he led out of Egypt, with whom he had made a covenant. The books of Exodus and Leviticus contain the first statement of this Law, given, according to the narrative, toward the beginning of the Exodus generation's journey out of Egypt toward the Promised Land. Deuteronomy is presented as Moses' farewell address, in effect, at the far side of their desert wanderings forty years later. This second statement of the Law is made to a new generation as they are about to enter the Promised Land under Joshua's leadership.

At the close of this statement, Moses promises that God will bring every blessing upon the people if they remain faithful to do what God instructed them. They will enjoy safety from the threat of attack by other nations. Their crops will be bountiful, their livestock increase, their families grow and prosper (Deuteronomy 28:1-14). But if they depart from God's Instruction to follow whatever ways seem best in their own sight, joining in the practices of the nations around them and failing to remain holy, set apart for God, God will punish them severely for their faithlessness. Their crops will dry up and their animals fail to conceive. Other nations will attack them, killing the inhabitants, plundering their lands, and dragging many off into exile in foreign lands (Deuteronomy 28:15-68). God would do all this because the people had forgotten all the good that God had done for them and failed to continue to live out a response of grateful obedience that would honor God, trampling on God's honor instead by their disobedience.

But there is always mercy with God. Beyond the experience of such curses, the people will remember God in exile. They will express sorrow for their unfaithfulness and return to God with all their hearts, intent on changing their lives and returning to an obedient, grateful lifestyle before God. When this happens, God will not leave them in the hands of their enemies, but will restore them to the security, independence, and prosperity that had been God's intent for them all along (Deuteronomy 30:1-14). The best course of action is therefore to choose obedience, which is to "choose life" (as opposed to its alternative) "by loving the LORD your God, by obeying his voice, and by clinging to him" (Deuteronomy 30:15-20).

The Lessons Applied

The books of Samuel and Kings are written from the perspective that the covenant blessings and curses played out consistently in the history of Israel and Judah. The author of Second Maccabees believes that more recent events continue to bear witness to these fundamental truths. He begins his story by noting the quality of life enjoyed by the nation under the high priest Onias III. Because Onias encouraged obedience to the

About the Text

Context and Shape of Second Maccabees

The author of Second Maccabees created his text by abridging an earlier, five-volume history (which means that it filled five scrolls) of the period by a Jew named Jason of Cyrene (see 2 Maccabees 2:23). This longer history has not survived. The facts of the history come from Jason, but they are given shape and interpretation by the author of Second Maccabees, who explains his purposes and method in the prologue (2:19-32) and epilogue (15:38-39) and who occasionally breaks into the story that he tells in order to underline the theological meaning of the events he relates (see especially 4:16-17; 5:17-20; 6:12-17; 12:43b-45).

In its present form, Second Maccabees begins not with this abridger's words, but with two letters. The first (1:1-10a) was written from authorities in Jerusalem to the Jewish community in Egypt in 124 B.C., encouraging them to join their Judean sisters and brothers in adding the festival of Hanukkah to their religious calendar (1:9). The second letter (1:10b–2:18) was written (if it is authentic) under the authority of Judas Maccabeus himself in 164 or 163 B.C., informing the Jewish community in Egypt of recent events and inviting them to celebrate the rededication of the Temple along with them (1:18). It appears that the Jewish authorities in Judea sent the letter of 124 B.C. with two "attachments": the earlier letter containing the first invitation and the abridged version of Jason's history (2:19–15:39) that, while not specifically written in support of the festival of Hanukkah, was certainly conducive to that purpose. This gave our Second Maccabees its present form. This also points to a date before 124 B.C for the composition of the body of the book.

covenant, the nation enjoyed peace and foreign kings even honored the Temple by underwriting the cost of sacrifices there (3:1-3). God watched over and protected the nation, providing supernaturally for national security. This is the reason behind telling the story of Heliodorus's attempt to inspect (and, no doubt, to raid) the Temple treasury on behalf of Seleucus IV, the Greek king ruling Syria, Babylonia, and Palestine (3:4-40). The people's and their leaders' devotion to the covenant was matched by God's commitment to make the promised blessings of Deuteronomy 28:1-14 a reality.

When Onias's brother Jason supplanted him, all this changed. Jason, backed by a significant portion of Jerusalem's elite, was not satisfied with life under the covenant. He wanted to make Jerusalem into a Greek city, to put it "on the map" of the larger, Greek world. With the permission of

Seleucus IV's brother and successor, Antiochus IV, Jason adopted a Greek constitution for governing the city of Jerusalem (replacing the Torah in regard to its civic legislation) and introduced Greek forms of education, athletics, and culture. The elite, at least, were forgetting the privilege, benefits, and obligation of worshiping the one God in the beauty of holiness, showing far greater enthusiasm for, and fascination with, what Greek culture and Greek connections had to offer. The author's voice intrudes upon his story again, warning that such an affront to God was leading to disaster for the city (4:16-17).

After Menelaus usurps Jason's place as high priest, Antiochus IV visits Jerusalem and does what Heliodorus had been unable to do—enter the Temple and carry off a great deal of its gold and silver (since Menelaus was significantly behind in tribute). The author's voice again interrupts to comment: the fact that Antiochus was able to do this was a result of the nation's increasing disobedience, which had caused God to withdraw his protection. If the leaders of the nation had remained steadfast in keeping the covenant, God would have driven off Antiochus just as he had done to Heliodorus (5:17-20).

The experience of the curses continues as the nation that Jason had courted not a decade earlier becomes a scourge that God would use to punish the nation, with tens of thousands of Jerusalem's residents being indiscriminately slaughtered. The Temple itself is defiled with pagan rituals and practices, as the people begin to worship other gods. Then something different happens. Living by God's Instruction is outlawed, and those who do try to continue to live in line with the covenant are persecuted and martyred by the high priest Menelaus and Antiochus's soldiers. Contrary to the latter's expectation, however, these people choose to remain obedient to the covenant and to God even to the point of being killed. The obedience they offer to God, the author will affirm, is the factor that turns the Deuteronomistic tables and turns the tide of history back in Israel's favor.

The lesson that the author wishes to communicate to his readers is clear: no path will bring advantage to the individual or to the nation if it leads away from covenant obedience. From a political point of view, it might indeed seem advantageous to meet the Gentile nation that enjoys power over God's people on its own ground and on its own terms. Blending in, doing what the members of the dominant group do, and trying to be more like the "winners" might very well seem like the path to enjoy what "they" have. In such situations, it is essential (the author would say) to remember what God has given God's people to enjoy and not to sacrifice the favor of the Creator of the cosmos for the sake of networking with those who enjoy temporary power.

The Martyrs and Their Sacrifice

The central episode in the first half of this book is the gruesome narrative of the martyrdoms of Eleazar, the seven brothers, and the mother of the seven (6:18–7:42). The author knows this is tough stuff, even preparing the readers for a scene that would surely be rated "R" for grisly violence and disturbing images (6:12-17). These nine characters endure the most brutal and inhumane torture rather than succumb to the pressure to renounce the covenant, symbolized by their agreeing to eat a mouthful of pork. They are martyrs because they bear witness ("martyr" comes from the Greek word *martys*, a word also applied to a witness in a courtroom). They testify in public to the value of the covenant and of maintaining their relationship and the nation's relationship to the covenant God. The Gentile king can make no promise so great that its enjoyment would be greater than enjoying God's favor. He can inflict no pain so terrible that it would seem better to avoid his torments and provoke God to anger.

The author presents their radical obedience as something that has value in God's sight beyond their individual cases. They themselves pray that the suffering they endure, suffering that they voluntarily undergo as the price of remaining obedient and thus offer to God, will suffice to bring God's punishment of the nation to an end (7:37-38). And, indeed, the author affirms that their voluntary deaths *did* bring God's anger to an end and restored God's mercy toward the nation (compare 7:38; 8:5). The martyrs' investment in the covenant is the turning point (as in Deuteronomy 30:1-11). Because of their willingness to suffer in obedience, the military hero, Judas Maccabeus, was able to begin to enjoy success on the battle-field. His campaigns would lead to the recapturing of the Temple and its cleansing, restoring it for the proper worship of the one God. They would eventually lead to the withdrawal of the Seleucid troops and the recognition of Judea as an independent, client kingdom under Judas's last surviving brother, Simon (see 1 Maccabees 14). The Jews once more "couldn't be defeated because they followed God's ordained laws" (8:36).

About the Christian Faith

Jewish Martyrs Inspired Early Christians

The story of the nine martyrs in 2 Maccabees 6:18–7:42 became increasingly important during the first three Christian centuries as the church faced heightening persecution and martyrdom. The author of the Letter to the Hebrews included them in his portfolio of what faith looks like in action (Hebrews 11:35). While the sons of the widow of Zarephath and the Shunammite woman were resuscitated and restored thus to their mothers (1 Kings 17:17-24; 2 Kings 4:18-37) only to die again, the Maccabean martyrs passed through death to the better, since endless, life of the resurrection by means of their steadfast endurance for God (see 2 Maccabees 7:9, 11, 14, 23, 29).

Origen (early Christian theologian and church father, A.D. 182–254) returned to these stories at great length in his *Exhortation to Martyrdom* as he urged two deacons to persevere in their Christian commitment when facing martyrdom under the emperor Maximin in A.D. 235. Cyprian of Carthage, writing his own *Exhortation to Martyrdom* a few decades later during a persecution by Valerian (A.D. 256), similarly used the stories of these Jewish martyrs to inspire Christians to pay the ultimate price for the sake of remaining loyal to God and holding onto the hope of life beyond death that God gives. The Maccabean martyrs would become the only non-Christian Jews included in the church's cycle of celebrating saints for having fought so courageously for God's sake even before Christ had overcome death's fearsomeness in his own resurrection (see Augustine, *City of God* 18.36).

An additional important contribution of these chapters is their testimony to a firm belief in the resurrection from the dead (7:9, 11, 14, 23, 29, 36). This hope is grounded in the dual conviction that obedience to the covenant leads to the enjoyment of long life and that God is absolutely just, such that God will not allow the individual righteous person to fail to enjoy the covenant blessings. Resurrection is God's vindication of the faithfulness of the righteous person: it proves that it is indeed better to die obedient than to secure a little more of this world's life through disobedience. It is also the vindication of God's faithfulness, proving that God remains faithful to those who are faithful, not allowing their oppressors to have the last word on their lives.

These two facets of the martyrs' story are an important background for how the early church began to make sense of the death of another righteous person and perhaps even for Jesus' own understanding of the significance of his death. The idea that one person's act of supreme obedience for the sake of the covenant could have redemptive benefits for the whole people of God clearly shows up in several key sayings of Jesus (like Mark 10:45; 14:22-24). Similarly Jesus expresses confidence that his voluntary death in obedience to God would lead to God's raising him from the dead (see Mark 8:31; 9:31; 10:33-34).

Live the Story

The New Covenant is not as clearly spelled out in its details as was the Old Covenant. Nevertheless, as we study the New Testament writings and the rich history of Christian formation we can get a fairly good sense of the contours of our part in keeping this covenant. It's not a question of "earning salvation"; it's a question of living as a responsible covenant partner with God, who will always keep his end of the bargain and will always make it possible for us to keep ours—if we seek God's help. For example, God will forgive our sins, as long as we forgive other human beings who have offended or hurt us. Does holding onto a grudge look better to us than forgiving? God promises us treasures in heaven if we invest our resources now in relieving the pressing needs of his people throughout the world. Does stockpiling money for the future or for luxury spending look better than helping someone who will die this week for want of food or help?

Our choices are not just private issues. They constitute a witness as well. If we forgive, if we share generously with brothers and sisters in need, this is a witness that God's covenant, favor, and promises are worth more to us than the self-gratifying or self-asserting alternatives. Where our fellow Christians in repressive nations face the same pressures as the martyrs in this text, our seeking ways to support them and their families, to lobby for their protection, and otherwise to stand alongside them is a witness to them that God's promises about the larger Christian family are reliable and a witness to the world about their innocent suffering.

Second Maccabees continues to call us, as it has called Christians for two millennia, to such covenant loyalty and such witness. In what ways does your own life and practice bear witness to the value of keeping covenant with God? Where is God calling you to grow into greater faithfulness in this regard?

4.

Fourth Maccabees

4 Maccabees 1–7; Galatians 5–6

Claim Your Story

When we hear a violinist give a virtuoso performance, or watch an Olympic gymnast perform an amazing sequence of movements, we are left in awe. To get to that moment, the violinist and the gymnast invested hours and hours every day, year after year, going through far more mundane exercises, developing each skill step-by-step, each routine motion-by-motion, in order to enable such a performance. They build up strength in the weight room so that they can achieve more on the stage or the court. They put themselves through all kinds of exercises and drills to hardwire habits into their bodies so that, when it comes time to perform, these actions and responses happen gracefully and perfectly without the need for conscious thought.

The person who wishes to excel in the Christian life, who wants to be a disciple in reality and not just in name, also needs to think about putting himself or herself through training exercises until certain actions or responses become habit and to work toward increasing moral and spiritual strength and stamina. One will no more wake up one morning a mature Christian than one will wake up able to play a Mozart concerto on the clarinet, unless one has practiced consistently and developed the skills and habits and deep comfort with the activity that comes from such intentional practice.

This is where the author of Fourth Maccabees connects with our story. He encourages us, if we wish to live in the high places of our walk with God and our witness for God, to discover and make full use of that divinely provided regimen for strengthening our moral faculty so that we will arrive at the goal of living beyond the power of our selfish desires and passions.

Enter the Bible Story

The author of Fourth Maccabees takes as his subject the stories of the martyrdoms found in 2 Maccabees 6:18–7:42, telling just enough of the backstory to set the stage. What we find in this book, then, is a kind of sermon on the martyrdom stories of Second Maccabees, prepared, it would seem, for an annual service commemorating their deaths (4 Maccabees 1:10). This is one of the most Greek of the books of the Apocrypha. The author had an excellent grasp of the Greek language, of Greek rhetoric and style, of Greek philosophy, and even of Greek literature. At the same time, it is also one of the most Jewish books. Everything the author writes is geared toward promoting continued commitment to the distinctive Jewish way of life laid out in God's Instruction, the Mosaic law. From beginning to end he affirms that God has given the Jewish people the ideal training program for attaining the highest moral character in terms that all Greek and Greek-educated people should be able to recognize and, it is hoped, learn to respect.

The Problem With the "Passions"

The author's thesis is that "God-centered thinking is supreme over emotions and desires" (1:1, my translation), a principle that recurs like a refrain throughout his sermon. Greek and Latin writers on ethics often took up the theme that "reason is able to master the passions." The word *passions* referred to a broad range of experiences that seemed to come upon a person's reason and will, attacking from outside, as it were. It included waves of emotions (like anger, fear, and pity), cravings and desires, urges and impulses, as well as physical sensations (whether painful or pleasurable). The CEB frequently translates the term as "emotions and desires" to keep reminding us of the range of meanings beyond simply stated "emotions."

As these Greek and Latin ethicists understood the human condition, these passions, if left unchecked, could overcome the rational mind and lead the individual to do things that were morally wrong, undermining his or her ability to choose the virtuous course of action. The emotion of fear or the sensation of pain could make a person act the coward, jeopardizing the greater good that is at stake. Greed (the craving for more) would work against the virtue of being generous toward those in need. Lust (the craving for physical, sexual pleasure) would work against the virtue of moderation and perhaps even justice (in regard to honoring marriage covenants). Envy works against justice, as envy drives people to prevent others from enjoying the rewards they deserve. Anger works against moderation and justice, driving people on to give others worse than they deserve or to lose sight of a higher good toward which people should be working together. Training the rational mind to keep the upper hand over the passions, therefore, became a central focus of Greco-Roman ethics, so that individuals could lead virtuous, well-disciplined lives and so that society could benefit from the same.

God's Training Program

The author of Fourth Maccabees agrees that the passions are a major impediment to living a consistently virtuous life and that proper moral formation involves the process of equipping the mind to master the passions so that the latter never get the upper hand in the decision-making process. He adds a twist to the familiar thesis, however, by naming specifically "God-centered" or "pious" thinking as the kind of rational process that enables the individual to master the passions (1:1; 6:31; 7:16; 13:1; 15:23; 16:1; 18:2; rendered as "clear thinking" at these points in the first printing of the CEB and better rendered as "godly thinking" in later editions). It is the mind that has been trained in God's Instruction (the Mosaic law) that is best equipped to master emotions, cravings, and other impulses (1:17). Living by this Law and internalizing its lessons allows the

Across the Testaments

Fourth Maccabees Illuminates the Torah

While Fourth Maccabees focuses most fully on the examples of the martyrs of 2 Maccabees 6:18–7:42, its author draws extensively on material from the Jewish Scriptures in the opening three chapters with a view to showing how the Torah trains people in the mastery of their urges and desires both by practical rules and by example.

Passage in Fourth Maccabees	Old Testament Resource	Interpretation of Old Testament Passage
4 Maccabees 1:33-34	Leviticus 11:4-23, 41-42; Deuteronomy 14:4-21	Laws limiting what Jews may eat, prohibiting certain succulent foods, exercises them in self-control.
4 Maccabees 2:1-4	Genesis 39:7-12	Joseph's story bears witness to the ability of the God-fearing to master sexual desires.
4 Maccabees 2:5-6	Exodus 20:17; Deuteronomy 5:21	The commandment against coveting proves that mastery of desires and urges is within the individual's grasp (contrast Romans 7:7-24!).
4 Maccabees 2:8-9	Exodus 22:25; 23:10-11; Leviticus 19:9-10; Deuteronomy 15:1-2, 9; 23:19-20	Commands concerning lending without interest, canceling debts every seventh year, and not going back a second time over one's crops after harvesting provide training against stinginess and greed.
4 Maccabees 2:10-13	Deuteronomy 13:6-11; Proverbs 13:23; 19:18; 23:13-14; 29:15, 17	The Torah trains the person to put justice ahead even of natural love for spouse or children.
4 Maccabees 2:14	Exodus 23:4-5; Deuteronomy 20:19-20	Specific commandments also train a person to overcome feelings of enmity and hatred.
4 Maccabees 2:17	Numbers 16:1-35	Moses' example proves that anger can be mastered.

Passage in Fourth Maccabees	Old Testament Resource	Interpretation of Old Testament Passage
4 Maccabees 2:19-20	Genesis 34:1-31; 49:7	Jacob's response to Simeon and Levi's anger proves that anger can be mastered.
4 Maccabees 3:6-18	2 Samuel 23:13-17; 1 Chronicles 11:15-19	David's example shows that proper fear of God can empower one to master powerful, irrational cravings.

rational mind to hold onto the reins and not allow the passions to drag it off into bad directions (2:21-23).

This is so, in part, because people who have been trained in God's Instruction think about all their choices in terms of their relationship with God. This puts their choices in perspective and makes it easier to choose the virtuous path, the path that honors that relationship, even when the immediate cost in terms of temporary safety or comfort is very high. They consider that they owe their very existence to God, such that it is only proper to use their bodies and capabilities fully in God's service as a way of honoring God's gift of life (13:13; 16:18-19). They consider that the God who gave them this life will also give life beyond death to those who keep faith with God (7:18-19; 16:25) and are thus more able to embrace short-term hardships for long-term advantages.

The mind trained in God's Instruction is also able to retain the upper hand over the passions because God has given people the perfect exercise program to train and strengthen the mind and will for such consistent mastery. The particular commands laid out in the Mosaic law constitute a regimen for exercising the will contrary to a person's selfish, self-centered, or self-indulgent cravings. Walking in line with God's Instruction (with the Law given through Moses) is not understood here in any way that resembles legalism or obsession with outward performance. It is understood as a formational process that works on the inner-most character of a person. By prohibiting the eating of pork or lobster, the Torah trained the pious Jew to curb her desire for succulent foods, teaching her to exercise self-control in small ways that would prepare for self-control in greater ways (1:31-35). By commanding the lending of money without interest and the cancellation of debts in the seventh year, the Torah trained the pious Jew to curb his greed and love for money, learning to support his neighbor's financial well-being against his own inclinations to acquire more for himself (2:8-9). Exemplary stories like Joseph resisting the advances of Potiphar's wife or Moses' restraint in dealing with his rivals taught the pious Jew to resist giving in to lust or anger (2:1-6, 16-18).

The power of the Jewish way of life to strengthen the rational mind and the will against being carried away by the passions is revealed climactically in the stories of the martyrs of 167–166 B.C., who allowed themselves to be tortured to death rather than break faith with the covenant. Defending the nobility of this way of life against the skepticism of the tyrant Antiochus IV, the martyr Eleazar says,

> You look down on our way of life as though living this way were unreasonable. However, our way of life teaches us self-control, so that we can have control over any pleasure or desire. It trains us to be brave, so that we willingly bear any suffering. It educates us about justice, so that it is always our custom to treat everyone fairly. It educates us in the godly way of life, so that we worship with due respect the only God who really exists (5:22-24).

This same training allows these Jews to remain true to their commitment to honor God and walk in God's ways rather than be defeated in their purpose by the tyrant's coercive tortures.

The road to moral consistency, even in the face of the most extreme internal or external pressures to act otherwise, is paved by means of a consistently disciplined life. The author values God's Instruction as outlining a way of life that exercises one regularly in ways both small and great that enable the individual to master the passions. The martyrs' example demonstrates the value of all the smaller victories over the passions—the regular, disciplined occasions for learning to master the passions whenever the Jew turns aside from scrumptious but forbidden food or curbs that inclination to go back over a field a second time to pick up the leftovers from one's harvest for oneself—that the Torah-led life inculcates. The author turns to the Law with the goal of discovering the freedom that the law-filled, disciplined life can bring.

The Holy Spirit, Our Personal Trainer

On this side of the coming of Jesus and of reading Paul, we would not tend to respond to the author of Fourth Maccabees by taking up the Jewish way of life. Paul takes the problem of the passions identified by the author of Fourth Maccabees with equal seriousness. Paul speaks of these in terms of the "selfish desires" or the "passions and . . . desires" that fight against God's work in us (Galatians 5:16-21, 24). But Paul would adamantly affirm that the Torah is no longer in place as God's exercise regimen for personal transformation. According to Paul, the quintessential Jew, that would be to turn back the clock on God's ongoing work of fulfilling his promise to

---

Maccabean Martyrs Appear in Christian Sermons

Even after persecution for the faith ceased to be a pressing danger for Christians—that is, after Constantine signed official edicts of toleration and even made Christianity the official imperial religion—church fathers continued to find the story of the Maccabean martyrs useful in their preaching. This was primarily thanks to the interpretation of that story already found in Fourth Maccabees, where the martyrs became the extreme example of the possibility of mastering the passions and desires of the flesh that interfered with embracing the virtuous course of action. In the Eastern Church, John Chrysostom devoted at least three sermons to these martyrs, preached on the occasion of the commemoration of the martyr-saints (August 1). He held up their courageous struggle in order to call his audience to "display as much endurance against the irrational passions—anger or desire for money, bodies, and fame—as they exhibited in their tortures" (*Homily 1 on the Maccabees,* 11). Their example should embolden Christians to "conquer the passions within us" and to "prune the unruly urges that course through our bodies" (*Homily 2 on the Maccabees,* 6). This was the theme also of Gregory of Nazianzus' sermon on Fourth Maccabees, urging his congregation to honor the martyrs by resisting their sinful passions and "fighting bravely against the daily Antiochus," namely sin, "that assaults us in every part of our body" (*Oration 15,* 12).[1]

Abraham to create a people for himself from many nations (Galatians 3:15–4:11). We are not relieved, however, of the need for the transformation of our persons from the inside out. Paul and the author of Fourth Maccabees share a fundamental conviction—to be most fully alive to God, we need to be most fully available to the virtuous inclinations and desires that God's Spirit plants within us. And we need to make room for these inclinations and desires by dying to the inclinations and desires that our untransformed self continues to cast up into our minds.

What Paul celebrates most about what Jesus has accomplished for us through his obedient death is that God's Holy Spirit is now freely available to everyone, Jew or Gentile. This is the inheritance, the promise, the unparalleled resource that God has given to people in Jesus (Galatians 3:14; 4:6-7). In place of the exercise videos and diagrams, God has sent a personal Trainer to work alongside us, to put us through the appropriate paces, to encourage us, even to empower us on the road to moral transformation, until the virtuous fruit of the Spirit ripens in and among us (Galatians 5:22-23). The good news of the gospel is not that God accepts us as we are and we don't have to worry about it. The good news of the gospel is that, wherever we are, God pours out upon us all that is needful for us to grow into the full stature of Jesus Christ, to become people of righteous character, desires, and life.

The spiritual disciplines practiced throughout the church's history have fulfilled much the same function as the Torah-driven life fulfilled for the author of Fourth Maccabees, creating spaces for the Spirit to work. Fasting in various forms, prayer vigils, or seeking simplicity of life are all practices deeply rooted in the Christian tradition that train us in little ways to master our drives and impulses so as to better equip us to master them in larger ways as well, when the pressures to give in to unholy drives are greatest. Reflecting upon and putting into practice specific instructions given to us by Jesus and by the apostles also work to change us, positioning us to fight against our selfish inclinations and urges.

Practicing these spiritual disciplines helps us train ourselves continuously to prioritize the life with God over the life of our natural inclinations, so that we discover ever-greater degrees of freedom in Christ from the passions and desires of the flesh, trusting that every small exercise trains us for faithful outcomes in greater trials. Our Western culture elevates self-gratification to the level of a core value or nonnegotiable good. The disciple who would grow in the knowledge and love of God must embrace all the more the countercultural heritage of the church, ordering his or her life around the spiritual disciplines that train our desires on God rather than toward the world's addictive, short-term painkillers.

Live the Story

Our story in Christ is one of a transformation so radical that it is best described in terms of dying to one set of prompts and coming alive anew to another set of prompts. We die to our self-centered cravings, to the feelings that prompt us to look out for ourselves at the expense of someone else or some greater cause. We come alive to Jesus' life surging up within us through the Holy Spirit, leading us to think, to want, to speak, and to do what is pleasing to God.

The author of Fourth Maccabees would ask us, where do *you* find those disciplines that enable you, through constant exercise, to master those urges and emotions that rise up within you, pulling you away from God's way, so that you can experience greater freedom and growth in the life with God? He would urge us to closer self-examination, to ask ourselves in the light of God's Word where we are driven by our less noble emotions and urges and what practices we need to take on to live more closely aligned with God's best vision for us. He would also encourage us that every step we take in this direction, no matter how faltering, prepares us— if we keep on stepping—to run and to dance one day in godly virtue.

1. My own translation.

5.

Prayers of Repentance in the Apocrypha

Prayer of Manasseh; Prayer of Azariah; Baruch 1:1–3:8

Claim Your Story

I've had occasion to be angry at God—*seriously* angry at God—at several points in my life. It was easy in those situations to blame God for what he did or did not do to keep me from experiencing heartache and pain or to keep me from suffering loss. I've had occasion to see close friends, colleagues, and parishioners in the same mode. God disappoints. God doesn't live up to his promises. God allows what is intolerable to come to pass. God fails us.

Several prayers in the Apocrypha invite us to consider, from a very different vantage point, how we have disappointed God, how we haven't lived up to our promises, how we have failed God. They invite us to consider the possibility that we have materially contributed to the intolerable coming to pass and to take responsibility as far as is appropriate (which is often far more than human beings are willing to admit to themselves). We may not be responsible for everything that hurts us (though that does not in itself make God responsible), but we, or those around us, may be far more responsible than we might imagine at first.

Calling us to self-examination and repentance, the authors of these prayers invite us to a much more honest inventory of blame and to remain connected with the God who is ever just, rather than allow bitterness to alienate us from the source of life and restoration.

Enter the Bible Story

Baruch, Prayer of Manasseh, and Prayer of Azariah are all set shortly before or after the conquest and destruction of Jerusalem at the hands of Nebuchadnezzar in 587 B.C. Baruch and Prayer of Azariah are written, as it were, from the place of exile, Babylon. Baruch was Jeremiah's assistant and scribe (see Jeremiah 36, for example) and came to be viewed as a leadership figure in his own right after Jeremiah's departure to Egypt. A later author takes on his persona and composes a liturgy of confession and commitment to return to God's ways (Baruch 1:1–3:8). The Prayer of Azariah is a similar prayer expressing sorrow for the people's sins and seeking reconciliation with God. After the original composition of the story of the men in the fiery furnace in Daniel 3, an editor placed this prayer on the lips of Azariah as a plea for deliverance (as well as inserting a lengthy song of praise, the Hymn of the Three Young Men, after their deliverance).

Manasseh was Judah's most wicked king. On his account, God's decree of devastation and exile would not be reversed even after the reign of godly Josiah (2 Kings 24:3). Unlike the story in 2 Kings 21, however, the story in 2 Chronicles 33 speaks of Manasseh himself being taken prisoner by the king of Assyria, acknowledging his wickedness there, and being restored by God. The chronicler refers to the text of Manasseh's prayer being preserved in the Annals of the Kings (2 Chronicles 33:18-20). This provided an opportunity for a later author to re-create, as it were, that prayer of repentance as a testimony both to the limitless mercy of God and to the place of self-examination, confession of sin, and heartfelt sorrow in the process of transformation. In so doing, he did not merely create a piece of historical fiction. Early Christians recognized Manasseh's prayer as the prayer of every soul before the Holy God, using it in their own liturgies.

These prayers all attempt to address the question "why do bad things happen to God's people?" And they all essentially use the historic setting of what was arguably the worst thing that happened to God's people as the context for working out their answers.

Taking Responsibility

These authors live in the shadow of Gentile domination of the people of God. Many Jews live outside of the land promised to them by God; those who do live in the homeland have experienced centuries of foreign rule, with Judah forming just one province in an empire. These authors project themselves back to the point in history when Judah lost its independence and the people—and the nation, its capital, and its Temple—suffered the trauma of conquest, devastation, and forcible removal to other lands.

It would have been easy, living in these conditions, to stay angry at God. *God, how could you do this to us? God, why have you not stood by your promises to your people? God, what is the use of serving you if we're not going to be protected from life's ills?* The authors of these prayers, however, have come to a place where they can start at a very different point:

> Justice is on the side of the Lord God, but public shame is upon us today, upon everyone in Judah, upon those living in Jerusalem, and upon our rulers, leading officials, priests, prophets, and ancestors, upon all of us who have sinned against the Lord. (Baruch 1:15-17; see also 2:6)

> Everything you've done to us is fair.
>> All your actions are right,
>> your ways consistent. . . .
> You judged us fairly
>> in all the things you've done to us
>> and to Jerusalem,
>> our ancestors' holy city . . .
>> because of our sins. (Prayer of Azariah 4-5)

> Now, Lord, I suffer justly.
>> I deserve the troubles I encounter. . . .
> I can't lift up my head
>> because of my sins. (Prayer of Manasseh 9-10)

The starting point of these prayers is that God is just, God is good, God is reliable. If we are experiencing adversity, it is not because of a flaw in God's character or judgment. A good place to start looking for blame *might* be with ourselves. Both Baruch and Prayer of Azariah are committed to the view of history expressed in Deuteronomy 27–32 (see session on Second Maccabees). According to this theology of history, the destruction of Israel and Judah and all the ills that followed were the result of the failure of God's people as a whole to live in line with God's covenant instruction. The problem was not that God was unjust, but that God was *perfectly* just and that the people, as a whole, deserved the consequences they suffered (Baruch 1:17–2:5, 7-10; Prayer of Azariah 5b-7, 9).

It is a point of humility to acknowledge God's justice, to hold fast to the conviction that God is in the right. *I* may not be in the right and may therefore need to submit myself to God's righteousness, learning from God where *I* have strayed from his desires for me. The blame does not, however, always fall on the sufferer: my *people* may not be in the right, and indeed sometimes the sins that we must confess are not our own individually, but those of our congregation, our denomination, our nation, or our race. My *circumstances* may not be right, such that I need to look for God's conforming these circumstances to his justice, the basis for the hope of the oppressed being that God is just and brings about justice. But *God* is always in the right.

This means that, when we find ourselves in the furnace we do not start by asking God, "God, what is wrong with *you*? How could you let this happen? What kind of God are you anyway?" Or if we do indeed *start* there in our anger or shock, we cannot stay there. When we come to the point where we can affirm, "God, you are in the right," then we can become open to hearing from God where the problem is and how to look for God's deliverance. If the problem is with us, we have confession and restoration; if the problem is with our people, we have prophetic witness and confrontation; if the problem is with our circumstances, we have hope in the God who hungers and thirsts for justice more fiercely than any victim of injustice.

Relying on God's Gracious Favor

These prayers challenge the stereotype of early Judaism as a religion of earning God's favor (and hence fostering self-righteousness based on

About the Christian Faith

Prayers of the Apocrypha in Worship Today

The Prayer of Manasseh and Prayer of Azariah have made important contributions to Christian worship for at least sixteen centuries. In a fifth-century Greek Bible, *Codex Alexandrinus*, a book called "Odes" follows the Book of Psalms. These odes are a collection of other biblical prayers and hymns from both testaments, brought together for convenience of reference for use as prayers in church alongside the Psalms. The Prayer of Manasseh, the Prayer of Azariah, and the Hymn of the Three Young Men are all included among these odes.

The Prayer of Manasseh continues to be used in Greek Orthodox worship, particularly in the service known as Great Compline, a service of confession and repentance used especially prior to and during the season of Lent. It also is printed in the Anglican and Episcopal prayer books as a canticle (a biblical prayer or hymn found outside the Psalms) during morning prayer. The Prayer of Azariah continues to be used in the Greek Orthodox service of Orthros, the daybreak service in the cycle of hours. The Hymn of the Three Young Men is also used in the service of Matins in Roman Catholic Liturgy of the Hours and in Anglican and Lutheran services of morning prayer.

"works"), of living under a constant threat of judgment, of proclaiming a harsh God of revenge and punishment. Yes, God is just. Yes, the covenant is to be lived. But God's favor precedes and infuses the covenant. God's mercy and kindness are core virtues as well. God's promises, which precede obligation (and broken faith), remain the basis for hope.

The authors of these prayers know that they, together with generations of their ancestors, can make no claim on God on the basis of their own righteous works.

> Lord our God, we are not basing our prayer for mercy on any righteous actions of our ancestors and rulers. (Baruch 2:19)

> Don't put us to shame!
> Instead, deal with us in line
> with your kindness and great mercy. (Prayer of Azariah 19)

These authors rely completely on God's tenderheartedness toward God's creatures, God's mercy toward those who come to realize how they've walked outside of God's good paths and are sorry for doing so. God's vast power, displayed throughout creation, poses a great threat to those who provoke God's anger by sinning against God's law (Prayer of Manasseh 1-5). But this same God is "kind, patient, and merciful," compassionate toward the sorrows that come upon humans, even when deserved (Prayer of Manasseh 6-7). This is the same language used when God reveals himself to Moses as "a God who is compassionate and merciful, very patient" (Exodus 34:6-7). One of the most powerful moments of God's self-revelation in the (Jewish) Scriptures is a word of hope to those who have failed to keep covenant with God.

Because God is both just *and* merciful, God gives sinners the opportunity to change their hearts and minds—in traditional language, to repent. By acknowledging what they have done wrong and expressing heartfelt sorrow for the consequences this has brought to their lives and their relationship with God, sinners find a point of connection with the "God of those who do what is right" (Prayer of Manasseh 8). The same God who is "God of those who do what is right" (Prayer of Manasseh 8) is also "God of those who turn from their sins" (Prayer of Manasseh 13). The God who created all people does not cease to be the God of those who fail in their covenant obligations, but stands ready to forgive and restore those who humble themselves and change their lives.

It is at this point that the choice of Manasseh as the speaker of this beautiful prayer of confession is most profound. Who is beyond repentance? Who has gone too far for God to be merciful, if he or she changes his or her heart and life? In the modern world, these questions usually elicit discussions of Stalin or Hitler. In the ancient world, a front-runner would have been Manasseh. The devastation of Judah and Jerusalem at the hands of Nebuchadnezzar's armies "happened to Judah because the LORD commanded them to be removed from his presence on account of all the sins that Manasseh had committed" several generations before (2 Kings 24:3). But even if Manasseh's sins and his multiplication of sins throughout the nation by his example and practice took the nation beyond the tipping point, even if the consequences of the covenant curses *had* to follow, no individual was beyond repentance and reconciliation (as 2 Chronicles

33:9-13 already taught). The wideness of God's mercy *indeed* rivals the breadth of the ocean.

Coming to the Place of Repentance

The author of Prayer of Manasseh asks for forgiveness using a beautiful image of humility: "Now I bend the knee of my heart, begging you to show kindness" (v. 11, translation mine). The author's outward posture—praying on his knees before God—is the exterior reflection of the attitude of his inner being toward God. The arrogance that he showed when he disregarded God's laws is gone, and he has returned to a proper attitude before the Life-giver. Both he and the author of Prayer of Azariah give eloquent expression to the heartfelt sorrow they feel as they grow in their awareness of how they have walked in paths that were destructive both of relationships with other people and of their relationship with God. Thus they lament:

> My sins are many, Lord; they are many.
> I am not worthy to look up,
> to gaze into heaven
>   because of my many sins. (Prayer of Manasseh 9)

> Accept us, please, with our crushed souls and humble spirits,
>   as if we brought entirely burned offerings of rams and bulls,
>   as if we brought tens of thousands of fat lambs. (Prayer of Azariah 16)

These prayers model for us the honesty and the humility that we are to have in God's presence about our own failings, and our utter dependence on God both for forgiveness where we have gone astray *and* for any progress that we make in growth as disciples. We, too, approach God recognizing that we don't stand among "those who do what is right," who don't need to repent, but among those who have sinned, to whom God offers the gift of changing our hearts and lives. In the despair of our own prison, or in the fierceness of our own furnace, we allow God's searching eye, and our own gaze, to look deeply within ourselves, to expose us as sinners. This allows us to have the humility of spirit to accept that

designation, so that we may also receive the deep forgiveness and reha-
bilitation that God longs to provide.

A Realignment of Our Purposes

The authors of all three prayers of repentance point to a larger con-
sideration than their own well-being as a motive both for prayer and for
God to act. Of course, Manasseh does not want to remain in prison in
Babylon, Azariah and his friends do not want to be burnt up, and Baruch
and his people do not wish to remain exiles forbidden to return to their
homeland. But they do not pray only for a happy resolution to each one's
own personal story but also for a crescendo in the telling of God's story in
the midst of a world that tends not to acknowledge God.

> For the sake of your own reputation,
>   please don't hand us over permanently!
>   Don't set aside your covenant! . . .
> As you have worked wonders before, so rescue us now!
>   Build up your reputation, Lord!
> Let all who mistreat your servants . . .
>   know that you alone are the Lord God,
>   more honored than anyone else in the world.
>   (Prayer of Azariah 11, 20-22)

> For your own sake, set us free and give us favor with those who have
> brought us into exile so that all the earth might know that you are the
> Lord our God, since Israel and her children carry your name.
>   (Baruch 2:14-15)

> In me you'll show how kind you are. (Prayer of Manasseh 14)

On the one hand, such statements can be read as the human being's
attempt to motivate God to respond, since God has as much at stake in
the situation as the one praying. God's power, goodness, and justice are
most visible in the lives of those who claim this God as their God. But
from another point of view, they express the humble acknowledgment of
a larger purpose. *Our* vindication is not the final issue. The vindication of

God's honor and God's reputation is the final issue. This is a mark of humility in that it maintains the proper order of things. As dependent beings, our lives are a means to an end; the honor of God, our infinite Creator, is that end. It is in this spirit that spiritual giants of the Christian tradition have always prayed, beginning with Jesus: "Hallowed be *thy* name."

Live the Story

Self-examination, confession, and heading in a new direction are hardwired into Christian worship and spirituality. Before receiving Communion, congregants pause to reflect on how they have lived for themselves rather than for God and for others, and pray for forgiveness and the gift of a changed life. When John Wesley crafted his Prayers for Daily Use to help disciples make greater progress in becoming Christ-centered and growing in particular Christian virtues, a major component was self-examination every morning and every evening.

Where do you engage these essential disciplines? One practice to consider would be to spend some time with the Ten Commandments, the Sermon on the Mount, or a section of Paul's (or another author's) instructions to the church and to ask: How have I walked in line with this vision for a just and holy life? When and where have I missed my step? What do I need to do to get on track in that area of life? Allow God to help you have the humility to really see yourself in light of this mirror, to name those missteps before God, and to feel the genuine sorrow that will help motivate a change of life. The prayers of Manasseh, Azariah, and Baruch assure us that we perform all such disciplines before a merciful God who longs to restore us.

6.

Sirach

Sirach selections

Claim Your Story

"Religion should only be taken so far. You also have to be a little practical." Though I chafed at this advice as a teenager, as it happens I've had no trouble following it. And I am surrounded by Christians who generally keep to an appropriate middle way between fanaticism and godlessness.

But every now and again I see—or even get to live out—a more single-hearted path. When living in line with God's or Jesus' or the apostles' vision for our transformation is going to be difficult and the practical voices clamor for moderating that vision and doing something else, sometimes we do choose the former. A woman who has been sensing a call to ministry finally breaks with her first career, simplifies her lifestyle, and answers that call. A family decides to use their vacation to become involved in a local mission, giving as much time and money to support homeless families as they gave to Disney the previous year. A man scales back his investment in corporate-climbing to have more time to give to his family and to his church's mentoring program.

Jesus ben Sira, compiler of the Book of Sirach, was a practical person who gave a lot of practical advice. But beneath all that advice is a steady drumbeat: *practical* never means "wise" if it involves not taking *God's* Instruction to heart and following it.

Enter the Bible Story

Jesus ben Sira was a scribe and sage who ran a private school in Jerusalem for the children of elite families. Like other such teachers and writers in the wisdom tradition, he sought to equip the young to achieve their full potential, to avoid common pitfalls, and to navigate their way successfully in every arena of life. Ben Sira also sought to implant values in his students, the foremost of which involved respecting the God of Israel and showing this respect in close observance of God's commandments. For him, living out these values was indispensable to being an honorable person. Nothing makes a person greater than this, and no honor lasts apart from this (Sirach 10:19-24).

While the pursuit of Wisdom led Ben Sira to read and adopt a great deal of material from Greek and Egyptian sages, he always remained centered in his own Jewish heritage, which is precisely where he found Wisdom herself to be most at home. Wisdom was present with God in creation and is evident throughout God's creation but is not accessible for all people. By God's order, Wisdom made her home among one particular people:

> The one who created me pitched my tent
> and said, "Make your dwelling in Jacob,
> and let Israel receive your inheritance." (Sirach 24:8)

She is to be sought in connection with the worship of God in the Temple (24:10-11) and, above all, "in the covenant scroll of the Most High God, the Law that Moses commanded us, the inheritance of the congregations of Jacob" (24:23; see also Baruch 4:1-4).

These were powerful, even prophetic words to proclaim between 200 and 175 B.C., when Ben Sira was likely active. At this time, many elite families were moving in a decidedly different direction as their path to increasing their honor, power, networks, and resources—the direction of accommodating themselves and their capital city to Greek culture and practices. Just a few short years after Ben Sira's death, the high priest Jason would reestablish Jerusalem as a Greek city with a Greek constitution and system of government (see 2 Maccabees 4), and both priestly and lay families would support him.

Ben Sira, witnessing the trend that would lead in that direction, applied himself to teach his students that, above all else, we find true wisdom when we walk in awe of God's majesty and in humble alignment with God's commandments.

From Hebrew to Greek

Ben Sira taught and wrote in Hebrew, but his grandson translated his collected wisdom into Greek for the benefit of Jews living in Egypt. Some of these Jews had lived for generations outside of their ancestral land of Judah. They had needed to learn and to speak Greek in order to interact with the people around them (Egypt had been part of Alexander's empire since 334 B.C.!) and had long since forgotten Hebrew and Aramaic. These Jews no longer read even their Scriptures in Hebrew, but depended upon Greek translations of the same. These are commonly referred to collectively as the Septuagint.

Ben Sira's grandson tried his best to represent his grandfather's meaning in Greek, but he asks his readers to "be forgiving in cases where we seem less than perfect in translating some expressions, despite working hard on the translation." He explains that "what was originally expressed in Hebrew does not have the same power when translated into another language. Not only in this case but even in the case of the Law, the Prophets, and the rest of the scrolls, there's no small difference between the translation and their expression in their own language" (Sirach Prologue 15-26). We need to remember that such differences between the original Hebrew text of the Old Testament and the Septuagint exist as we read the New Testament, for most early Christian communities embraced the Septuagint as their Old Testament Scripture.

While we depend primarily on the Greek version of Sirach, portions of copies of the Hebrew text have been discovered among the Dead Sea Scrolls and in the ruins of Masada. Further, partial medieval manuscripts were found in a storage room in a synagogue in Cairo. The CEB reflects the differences between these versions throughout in the footnotes.

Wisdom Through Commitment (Sirach 1–2)

Wisdom meant, essentially, living intelligently, making advantageous choices, finding the way to make the most out of life by avoiding common pitfalls (whether typical mistakes people make or deeper character flaws). The path to gaining advantage, however, was debated in Ben Sira's setting. Was the old, traditional way of life laid out in God's Instruction holding Jerusalem and Jewish families back from getting the most out of life?

For Ben Sira, wisdom was always to be found where reverence for God ("fearing the Lord" by honoring God's Instruction) was the first and the last word (Sirach 1:14-20, 26-27). As he would remind students later, "All wisdom involves doing the Law" (19:20).

Attaining genuine wisdom and its fruit would require two key qualities: sincerity and commitment. Wisdom is not a commodity; it is the result of a relationship with an all-knowing, all-perceiving God. Therefore, the seeker's heart has to be "right." This means single-hearted commitment to following the path that God laid out and confidence that this path does indeed lead to God and God's rewards—rewards, moreover, that are greater and longer-lasting than any offered by following some other path. The greatest enemy to success is the "divided heart" (1:28), which leads to a person trying to walk "two paths" (2:12), the path of God's Instruction and some other, quicker path to short-term benefits. As James would put it much later, trying to be friends with the world and friends with God at the same time, so as to benefit both ways, just doesn't work (James 4:4).

Ben Sira knows that trying to align oneself and one's life with God's Instruction is difficult, that it requires a lot of discipline and a lot of deferral of rewards. This is why he likens it to being tested as gold melted down in the furnace: the process shows up any impurities like insincerity, a lack of commitment, a divided desire. Wisdom and her promised benefits come only after a "long obedience in the same direction" (Friedrich Nietzsche, *Beyond Good and Evil*, 5.188).

Wisdom for Living (Sirach 27:30–29:13)

Most of Ben Sira's book focuses on providing sound advice for all kinds of domestic, social, economic, and political situations. Some of this is just common sense (and some is, admittedly, not so helpful). At many points, however, Ben Sira's advice is theologically grounded in ways that would remain persuasive for centuries and would come to be incorporated into Christian wisdom as well, including the wisdom taught by Jesus, James, and Paul.

One such area focuses on harboring anger and unforgiveness. Ben Sira knows these to be destructive forces in human community and cautions against both. He does so by putting how we relate to one another in the context of how God relates to us. Do we, being mere human beings, think offenses against us are unforgiveable? How could we, then, presume that God should forgive our offenses against him, when his honor, which we have abused when we act without regard for his commands, is infinitely greater than our own? If we insist on getting even when we've felt slighted, we're in for a rude awakening when God, who has endured worse slights from us, his own creatures, comes to judge (Sirach 28:1-7; see Matthew 6:9, 14-15).

A second such topic focuses on what we do with our extra money. Do we hoard it to keep for ourselves for some future time when we might or might not need it? Or do we invest it in our neighbors, whom we are to love as ourselves, giving loans to those who are worse off than we are or giving charity to the poor among us? Ben Sira teaches that those who spend their extra cash in the latter manner are the ones who are really laying up a treasure that can help them in their future distress, since they are investing in accordance with God's commandments (Sirach 29:8-13; see Matthew 6:19-20; Luke 12:33-34). There is one point here at which Jesus ben Joseph, our beloved Savior, will challenge the classical sage. Ben Sira instructs his students to give their charity only to the righteous poor, on the double ground that wicked people will only hurt their benefactors and that God also hates sinful people (Sirach 12:1-7). Jesus, however, knows a God who gives his gifts to the just and unjust alike, and urges his disciples to reflect such perfect, complete generosity in their own giving (Matthew 5:43-48).

Wisdom Through Awe (Sirach 42:15–43:33)

Sages did not always keep their noses in scrolls or remain debating inside four walls, though they did invest themselves plenty in both pursuits (Sirach 38:34b–39:11). Wisdom was not just to be read about, but it was also to be observed; it was to be intuited. Ben Sira spent time outdoors, perhaps sitting on his own rooftop to watch the sun rise and make its light glisten and dance upon the city and the landscape around him. He stared at the night sky, drinking in the awesome wonder of its beauty and immensity. Wherever he looked, he saw the handiwork, the wisdom-in-action, of the Creator. Perceiving nature as creation opened him up to the experience, no doubt time after time, of allowing awe at the majesty of the earth and the heavens to become a pathway to experience awe at the power, wisdom, and intelligence of the God whom he served (see also Sirach 1: 1-9).

The author of Wisdom of Solomon also believed that contemplation of the natural order ought to lead to discovery of the character of the Creator. Most people, however, failed to make this leap, and ended up worshiping the stars and planets instead: "Though they were fascinated by what [God] had made, they were unable to recognize the maker of everything" (Wisdom 13:1-2). Paul would later say much the same thing (Romans 1:18-23). Ben Sira, however, could see "God's invisible qualities—God's eternal power and divine nature" (Romans 1:20) through their reflection in creation. This set him in awe before the creator God and renewed him in humility to walk in line with God's ordering, not only of the cosmos, but of the life of God's people through his Instruction.

Across the Testaments

Ben Sira's Wisdom Carried in the New Testament

Ben Sira was in a strong position to impact the leaders of the early Christian movement. A champion of Torah observance who ran a respectable school in Jerusalem two centuries before Jesus' birth, Ben Sira preserved his wisdom in writing. Fragments of his book were found among the Dead Sea Scrolls and in the ruins at Masada. He is quoted in rabbinic texts no fewer than eighty times. While he was not considered the writer of inspired Scripture, he was certainly regarded as a worthy teacher and conversation partner broadly within Judaism. Jesus, Paul, James, and other leaders of the new messianic movement no doubt had many opportunities in the synagogues of Nazareth, Tarsus, and Jerusalem to encounter Ben Sira's wisdom. The following table shows some major points of positive influence.

Passage in Sirach	Passage in the New Testament	Major Points of Positive Influence
Sirach 4:4-5, 10	Matthew 5:38-45	Ben Sira urges giving to the person in need; providing for and protecting the vulnerable shows one to be "a child of the Most High."
Sirach 28:1-5	Matthew 6:12, 14-15; 18:23-35	We must forgive those who who have offended us if we hope for God to forgive our offenses against God.
Sirach 29:9-12	Matthew 6:19-20; 19:21; Luke 12:33-34	Charitable giving is a better way to lay up a treasure against future need than to hoard it, letting it rot rather than do good.
Sirach 51:23-27	Matthew 11:28-30	A wisdom teacher invites disciples to come under his yoke and find rest after little labor.
Sirach 7:5, 8-9	Luke 18:10-14	No one, no matter how pious or how generous in supporting the Temple, should be presumptuous in regard to sinning and being forgiven by God.
Sirach 1:30; 3:18	Matthew 23:12; Mark 10:42-44; Luke 14:11; 18:14	Exalting one's self leads to being humbled by God; those who are great must humble themselves to find God's favor.
Sirach 33:10-13	Romans 9:19-24	As their Creator, God has the right to do with human beings as God pleases, like potters have absolute authority over their clay and handiwork.
Sirach 2:1-6	James 1:2-4; 1 Peter 1:6-7	When people draw near to God, testing through adversity follows. This gives an opportunity for developing steadfastness and demonstrating one's commitment.

Passage in Sirach	Passage in the New Testament	Major Points of Positive Influence
Sirach 15:11-20	James 1:13-15	God does not test people, leading them astray; we are tempted and misled by our own desires and urges.
Sirach 19:16; 22:27; 28:12-16	James 3:6-12	Speech is as dangerous as fire; it is to be carefully kept in check, and not allowed to spew forth both blessings and curses.
Sirach 14:2	1 John 3:21-22	Those whose consciences are clean can have confidence of God's favor.

Wisdom Through Worship (Sirach 50:1–51:13)

Perhaps the most famous passage of Ben Sira's is his hymn in honor of the Hebrew ancestors (Sirach 44:1–49:16), celebrating the lasting, praiseworthy remembrance won by those who were faithful to God's covenant, especially those who also enjoyed the particular honor of priesthood. This hymn climaxes in Ben Sira's praise of the recently deceased high priest, Simon II (50:1-24). While he remembers Simon's excellence as a civic leader (50:1-4), he is especially struck by the memory of having seen Simon in action in the Temple (50:5-21).

Although Ben Sira is often thought to be describing part of the Day of Atonement ritual, he is more likely remembering the splendor of the everyday whole burnt offering and its accompanying rites (the pouring out of wine, the offering of incense) under the leadership of this model priest. Simon knew and communicated well what it meant to "worship the LORD in the beauty of holiness" (Psalm 96:9, KJV). Ben Sira's description challenges any of our stereotypes of Temple worship as a matter of "going through the motions" for the Jews who participated and witnessed. The ritual clearly stirred up deep feelings of the awesomeness of God's presence and the experience of interacting intimately with God through the liturgy. This, in turn, should challenge any prejudices we harbor against the value of liturgical worship in the Christian tradition, as well.

For those who think that Judaism was just about performing the outward rites and sacrifices, Ben Sira strikes hard against those prejudices as well. God will accept only that which was acquired in justice, and not through exploiting the poor or taking advantage of one's workers, as an offering or sacrifice (Sirach 34:21-27; 35:14-15). People should present their gifts to God in the Temple joyfully, in response to God's generosity toward them (35:10-13); but God is even more interested in their obedience to the values of the covenant day after day. Thus God regards the person who shows generosity toward others, especially toward the poor, as having made a good offering to God as well (35:1-5). Rituals and ethics go hand-in-hand and are mutually reinforcing.

Finally, Ben Sira's own original prayers (51:1-12; see also 36:1-22) show us a man of prayer and devotion. Participation in the Temple rituals went hand-in-hand with a deep, personal awareness of God and the ability to connect with God in personal prayer fueled by liturgical worship. Ben Sira's example challenges some modern prejudices that liturgical worship and ritual stifles, rather than nurtures, personal devotion and piety.

Live the Story

Perhaps the essence of Wisdom, according to Ben Sira, is to remember who God is, and who you are. This remembering is not an act of our minds so much as an ongoing renewal of our experience of awe before God, both as we take time to stand before the majesty of God's handiwork in creation and as we enter to "worship the LORD in the beauty of holiness" (Psalm 96:9, KJV). Awe reorients us. It brings an ongoing rediscovery of God's power, wisdom, and well-ordered beauty. It moves us to recommit ourselves to walk in humility and in alignment with God's Instructions.

Wisdom, born of this awe before God, grows by trusting the instruction that God has given as an act of extreme kindness on God's part, showing us a way to live that bears fruit in our relationships, our communities, and within our own souls beyond what the path chosen by the practical mind could yield. For Christ-followers, this instruction would now include

Jesus' teachings and the words of his emissaries, the apostles and their teams, and as Jesus ben Joseph would say, the wise person is the one who builds his or her life upon and around Jesus' teachings (Matthew 7:24-27). Living wisely results from a single-hearted commitment to do what God commands, even when the results would be deemed impractical.

7.

Wisdom of Solomon

Wisdom 1–5

Claim Your Story

A woman invests herself fully in making partner in a prestigious law firm, shutting out opportunities for love and family. A church makes little or no impact on its community because its members devote their time, energy, and resources to their own work and to enjoying their "fair share" of leisure activities and other indulgences. A couple moves toward divorce because each partner is focused on how he or she is not getting what she wants out of the marriage and feeling life slipping away. A man tosses out the junk mail from World Vision and Voice of the Martyrs appealing for support and puts a glossy brochure for the new BMW M6 on his dresser.

We are inundated with messages about what we should value and try to get out of life. We are told that we have a right, even a duty, to gratify ourselves and to be fulfilled, and to measure our commitments accordingly. But all such messages come from a world that has made a "treaty with death" (Wisdom 1:16), whose structures are built up around the cardinal values of consumerism and accumulation, and that drives us to think of *this* life as the primary arena where we will be fulfilled or die the losers.

Enter the Bible Story

Solomon was famous for his wisdom, becoming a kind of patron saint of sages. Several authors who wrote much later than Solomon were attracted to his name and they sought to attach their own work to his tradition. So it is with the Wisdom of Solomon. This book is attributed to Solomon and, to some extent, written from Solomon's point of view (see Wisdom 7:1–9:18, which echoes Solomon's prayer in 1 Kings 3:1-15), but really comes from the time of the early Roman Empire. A Greek-educated Jew, probably living in the large Jewish community of Alexandria, Egypt, wrote it.

The book essentially tells three stories: the story of the ungodly who live to satisfy their own urges and oppress the righteous person who bears witness to something greater (1:12–5:23); the story of a political ruler's quest for Wisdom (6:1–9:18); and the story of Wisdom's activity in guiding God's people, particularly in the Exodus (10:1–19:22). The first of these stories will be our focus in this session.

Living for This Life Only

The author of Wisdom of Solomon had some brilliant insights into human psychology. Foremost is his reflection on how our perception of death can distort our lives, changing us from the kind of being God sought to create into self-serving animals. If we look ahead to death as truly the dead end of our existence, as more of a brick wall into which we slam at life's end rather than as a doorway to further existence in God's presence, our gaze may be turned back upon our lives here in a most unhealthy manner. The "now" can be magnified to such a degree that our whole view of life, relationships, and purpose becomes distorted.

Thus the author imagines people whose self-talk includes statements like "our lives are short and painful. There is no antidote for death; no one has come back from the grave" (Wisdom 2:1). "All of us came into being by chance" (2:2). "Over time, our names will be forgotten" (2:4). "This life is all we have" (2:9). If we can't see past our own deaths—at the very least in terms of leaving an honorable memory (2:4)—we stand in danger of doing great harm by living essentially self-centered and grasping lives. If we don't grasp God's purpose for our lives (2:2, 22), we will invest ourselves in the illusions of purpose that we devise for ourselves. The author sees such a view of life leading to a commitment to "enjoy all the good things of life now," to "enjoy creation to the fullest as we did in our youth" (2:6). For such people, making "the most of this life" (2:9) means indulging themselves to the extent that their resources permit. Perhaps this does not show up specifically as "expensive wines," "fine perfumes," and plucking "every fresh blossom of spring" (2:7), but it does show up wherever consumerism is rampant, wherever getting what appeals to us at the moment drives our choices and investments. This is "twisted" reasoning, according to Wisdom of Solomon (2:1).

A self-centered consumerism (that notably leaves a destructive footprint on creation; see Wisdom 2:7b, 9) is not the worst outcome of such thinking. Obsession with the importance of one's own enjoyment of this life to the fullest ("making the most of this life") leads to preying upon other human beings, robbing them of their enjoyment of this life (2:10). Such a mindset leads overtly to a "might makes right" ethic (2:11), wherein the weak are devoured to satiate the immoderate cravings of the powerful. Virtue, which often takes its starting point from measuring the value and the needs of the other, no longer motivates such people's actions. We see this wherever a higher value is placed on profit than on the well-being of real people, wherever self-gratification on the part of those with power trumps thinking about how to meet another person's needs.

In a final step toward depravity, such people use their power to abuse and kill those whose lives bear witness to higher values, whose speech and actions are a constant challenge to their cosmology, namely, their place at the center of their universes (2:12-20). It becomes essential for them to try to disprove the faith convictions of the God-centered person: "Let's put him to the extreme test and see what happens" (2:17); "Let's condemn him to a disgraceful death: according to him, God should show up to protect him" (2:20). And when they are successful in killing the righteous person, they feel vindicated that they have the right view of the world after all and can go on doing as they've done.

This is not true for everyone, of course. For some people, awareness of mortality can lead to greater care in how they spend their limited time upon this earth, prioritizing relationships over acquisition, giving their short span meaning through living up to higher ideals, becoming more humane and humble in the face of our shared mortality. But where we do not hold securely to the hope for life with God beyond this life, the author of Wisdom of Solomon warns us that we also stand in danger of degenerating into something far less than human, becoming merely the cleverest of beasts.

This author spoke of such a mindset as making a deal, a "treaty," with death (1:16), as if to say, "Since you're going to have the final word, Death, I'll be happy just to get all I can out of this life." There are so many ways by which Death can take us captive through such deals. The desire to escape from death can take the form of moment-to-moment escapes through drugs, shopping, eating, or sexual encounters. The feeling that our lives are slipping away can easily drive us to act in our own interests rather than those of others, often those closest to us. Awareness of death can also drive us to pursuits that we think will insulate ourselves against death. In the ancient world, Egyptian kings built their pyramids as, essentially, illusory replacements for immortality. The pyramids can still be seen, bearing witness to the longevity of the illusion, though they have not given life to their builders. The same fear of death can drive us to climb nearer to the tops of our corporate pyramids, or to build large homes and surround ourselves with "stuff" as if these provided effective insulation against death. In this way, our limited time and energy are siphoned off from investments that have lasting value in God's sight for trivial pursuits.

Eternity and Ethical Potential

According to the author, Death's power to drive and to distort people's lives, relationships, and investments of themselves comes from making a fundamental error: "They didn't know of God's secret plan. They didn't hope for the reward that holiness brings" (Wisdom 2:22). In other words, they didn't understand that "God created humans to live forever," that immortality was part of the package of being made in God's image (2:23). This is certainly a faith claim on the author's part, though the opposite line of reasoning was no less driven by faith claims about the nature of our existence ("all of us came into being by chance"; "this life is all we have" (2:2, 9). The author's faith claim, moreover, proves to be superior in at

Paul Uses Wisdom of Solomon

Wisdom of Solomon, a product of Greek-speaking Judaism, exercised a formative impact on Paul and his team. As a Pharisee, Paul looked forward to the resurrection of the dead in some embodied form (see 1 Corinthians 15). Deeply influenced by Greek-speaking Judaism, however, he also speaks of human existence in terms of a soul—the spiritual essence of a person, in effect—inhabiting a body and looking forward to its release. Both Paul and the author of Wisdom speak of the body as an earthly tent that, in some sense, weighs down the soul that is the real person (Wisdom 9:15; 2 Corinthians 5:1, 4). The author of Wisdom sharply criticizes the Gentile world's failure to recognize and worship the creator God, worshiping facets of the material creation instead, from sun and planets to idols crafted from wood and stone. He believes that this essential failure lies at the root of the social, personal, and moral chaos polluting human civilization (Wisdom 13:1-9; 14:22-31). Paul would take up all of these topics, in the same order, in his indictment of the Gentile world before God (Romans 1:18-32), though he would go on to turn the tables on his fellow Jews as well because of their own disobedience (2:1-11).

We find an even more profound impact on Colossians and in Hebrews, the second of which was written probably not by Paul but by one of Paul's ministry colleagues. Wisdom of Solomon draws upon Proverbs' presentation of Wisdom as a superhuman figure present with God, and working alongside God, in creation (Proverbs 8:22-31), and goes further. This figure of Wisdom is not only "the skilled fashioner of all" but "a breath of God's power and a spotless mirror of God's power to act and an image of God's goodness" (Wisdom 7:22, 25). Paul and the author of Hebrews seize upon *this* language to begin to talk about the being and activity of the Son before he took on flesh (see Colossians 1:15-20; Hebrews 1:1-4). Intertestamental reflection on Wisdom provides the raw material for early Christology.

least this regard: it enables us, as human beings, to live in line with what humans have recognized as virtuous for millennia and to rise above the self-seeking tendencies that drag us down below the level of animals.

Furthermore, reading Wisdom of Solomon from the point of view of the Christian Scriptures gives us one major, additional reason to take the author's side in this debate. Someone has indeed come back from the grave (contrast Wisdom 2:1). That same someone has further demonstrated that God's vindication does not need to happen within the confines of this life, but that God is free to intervene on behalf of the righteous at any point in this life or after death (contrast Wisdom 2:17-20). And the good news about Jesus' resurrection is that it is just the beginning of the general resurrection of the dead, the down payment on our own resurrection (see 1 Corinthians 15:20-22).

The author of Wisdom of Solomon believed in the immortality of the soul, the essential part of ourselves that makes us who we are, animates our bodies, allows us conscious experience. This meant, for him, that the wise person would not live with a view to what seems advantageous for this life only, but what would be advantageous for eternity. This meant, in turn, that living with a view to pleasing God, whose opinion would count for eternity, would always be the most advantageous path, even if it meant enjoying less of this world's goods (or all-out loss). Indulging one's every wish or want suddenly pales alongside making sure people in need enjoy what is necessary for life. Using one's power to enrich one's self at the cost of the less powerful suddenly appears foolhardy, in contrast to using one's power to protect the interests and enhance the lives of weaker neighbors. Rather than persecuting those who bear witness to God, those who have hope for eternity find themselves standing alongside those who are thus mistreated, encouraging them in prayer, in the sharing of resources, and in political action on their behalf.

Hoping for immortality (or belief in our own resurrection) frees us from death's power to distort our lives and empowers us for ethical action, even when the latter is costly in terms of our own enjoyment of this world's goods. It directs us away from the dead end of thinking that we need to get all we can out of this life, no matter what this costs those around us. It frees us from investing all our time and energy and resources in those pursuits that give us the illusion of being insulated against death and oblivion, and allows us to invest our time, energy, and resources instead in that which will indeed last for eternity. In one sense, "virtue is what will be remembered, and this means immortality" (Wisdom 4:1). Those who live for this life only come to realize that they've fulfilled their own grim predictions for life. They have indeed vanished as though they had never been, leaving no remembrance, because they "leave behind no evidence of virtue" and, instead, "squandered what [they] had in bad living" (5:13).

About the Christian Faith

Early Christians See Jesus in Wisdom of Solomon

Wisdom of Solomon's development of the figure of Wisdom and her relationship to God would continue to feed early Christian theologians' reflections on the relationship of the Father and the Son within the Trinity through the first four centuries of the church. Wisdom 7:22–8:1 was an important text in discussions leading to the affirmation that the Father and the Son were equal and shared the same essence (as in the line from the Nicene Creed, "of one Being with the Father") and that the Son was (again from the Nicene Creed) "eternally begotten of the Father" as light is perpetually begotten of fire. Quodvultdeus (*On the New Song* 7.1-17) affirmed that the Son displayed the same omnipresence and omnipotence as the Father, since the Son (as Wisdom) "reaches in strength from one corner of the earth to the other, ordering all things well" (Wisdom 8:1).[1] At the same time, the unity of Father and Son was argued on the basis of their being no more two distinct entities than light's radiance is an entity distinct and separable from the light source (Ambrose, *On the Christian Faith,* 1.7.48-49; Augustine, *Tractates on the Gospel of John* 20.13; *On the Trinity* 4.20.27).

Wisdom of Solomon's description of the testing and shameful execution of the righteous person by the ungodly (Wisdom 2:12, 17-20) also attracted considerable attention as a prophecy about Jesus. The description of the righteous person as God's son, and the imposition of a shameful death upon this person in connection with that claim (Wisdom 2:13, 16), led Christians to read it in light of Jesus' story (see Origen, *Homilies on Exodus* 6.1; Augustine, *City of God* 17.20; *Expositions on the Psalms* 48.1.11).

But in a more ultimate sense, those who live virtuously will live in God's presence forever (3:1-9; 5:15). Life was a test (3:5-6), and they passed because they understood the questions and the criteria for evaluation. That test comes in each moment in which we must choose between looking out for our own interests and looking out for God's interests in a given situation, which generally means looking out for another person's good. The promise of immortality frees the individual to choose the latter, to understand that there is no greater good that one can gain for oneself in the years of this life than doing that which is good in the sight of the one who has power to grant eternity. Those who are shortsighted use this life to invest in the rewards of this life, by any means necessary. Those who are wise use this life to invest in the rewards of eternity, in keeping with God's Instruction. There is a way for our lives to amount to something more than strutting and fretting our hour upon this stage, to be heard from no more. As the seventeenth-century Anglican priest, John Donne, put it so well: "upon every minute of this life depend millions of years in the next, and I shall be glorified eternally, or eternally lost for my good or ill use of God's grace offered to me this hour."[2] Donne's goal was not to arouse anxiety, but to help his congregation see the significance of each hour of this life. Living for this life only is the product of failing to recognize this significance. The result is that the common manner of trying to "make the most out of life" ends up making the least out of life, for it does not make the most of this life *for eternity*.

Live the Story

How does our awareness of our mortality affect us? Does it subtly (or not so subtly) drive us to try to leave some mark on the world or some monument to our having been here as a means of trying to cheat mortality? Does it drive us to value our own fulfillment and gratification in the time that remains to us more than pouring ourselves into fulfilling others? How do these impulses affect our ability to be responsive to God and to give of ourselves, as God would have us?

The author further challenges us to decide whether there is indeed a God-directed purpose for our lives—one that lifts us above living for ourselves and this life only—and to trust in this purpose enough to invest ourselves fully in it by giving away our lives for others and for God's goals for human community. And if we do, what do we need to change in our attitude toward relationships, work, spending, and the like so as to build our lives more fully around living for eternity rather than living for this life only (or primarily)? The author of Wisdom of Solomon was able to orient himself toward eternity; how much more should we be able to do so now that one *has* come back from the grave to tell us that death is an open door.

1. My own translation of this verse.
2. John Donne, sermon XXXVII, "Preached on Trinity Sunday," *The Works of John Donne: With a Memoir of His Life*, Volume 2, 160.

8.

Judith

Judith 8–16

Claim Your Story

"What can *I* do about it?" As we contemplate some of our world's daunting ills—the violence ravaging African villages, the tens of thousands dying from lack of food each day, the violence in our own inner cities, the rise in unemployment and homelessness, the ecological changes that threaten the future of our kind—we often feel like grasshoppers at the feet of giants. But every now and then someone asks, "What can *God* do about it through me?" Christine Caine asked this question in regard to human trafficking in 2007. She and her husband Nick committed themselves to this cause, taking time and energy from many other activities, with the result that they now spearhead the A21 Campaign, a nonprofit, nongovernmental organization that has mobilized over 4,500 people to become actively involved in ending the modern slave trade. They have raised up a giant force to combat a giant evil. The world's daunting ills are giants to us, but not to God, who can do great things through ordinary women and men willing to put themselves at God's disposal.

Enter the Bible Story

The figure of Judith does not actually appear in the book bearing her name until almost halfway through the story, as the story begins to move from complication to resolution. The crisis that provides her with her opportunity to shine is an invasion of a vast foreign army led by

Nebuchadnezzar's right-hand general, Holofernes. Nebuchadnezzar had been waging a war against the powers to the east and had demanded that his western allies (as far as Egypt) send him soldiers to assist. These nations, however, did not respond, showing contempt for Nebuchadnezzar. After his conquest of the east, Nebuchadnezzar sent his armies to avenge his injured honor by subduing the western nations, reminding them of their place in the food chain, as it were.

There is a grander honor contest at work in this story, however, one that ultimately spells doom for Nebuchadnezzar. The Babylonian king waged a war not only against the nations that had dishonored him, but against their gods as well. As Holofernes cut a swath through the western rebels, he "demolished all their shrines and cut down their sacred groves. He had been commanded to destroy all the gods of the land so that all the nations would worship only Nebuchadnezzar, and so that those of every language and tribe would call upon him as their god" (3:8; see also 4:1-2). When Holofernes is told about the God of Israel who protects his people as long as they are faithful to the agreement he made with them, he all but challenges this God to a duel: "Who is god except Nebuchadnezzar? He will send his power and destroy them from the earth, and their God won't rescue them" (6:2b).

This invasion force bears down on the imaginary hill town of Bethulia, which controls a pass through the mountains. As long as the citizens of Bethulia hold out, Holofernes will not be able to march his army through to Jerusalem to carry out his master's commands regarding its Temple's desecration and destruction. As we read the story from this point, we need to keep in mind all that is at stake here, for it puts into perspective the consequences of the town's surrender and the lengths to which Judith goes to protect God's honor as well as deliver her town.

By the Hand of a Woman

The Book of Judith stands in the biblical tradition of celebrating God's ability to give victory to the weaker party in the face of significantly more powerful adversaries (see Judith 9:11). In Deuteronomy, Moses tells the people not to be alarmed when they see the chariots and cavalry of the

Finding Truth in Fiction

The Book of Judith is a piece of historical fiction. The story plays out against the backdrop of known characters and events (like Nebuchadnezzar and his invasion of the lands west of Babylon), but the story itself is not historical. A dead giveaway that the author is writing fiction is the impossible setting of Holofernes's invasion. This is said to happen at the instigation of Nebuchadnezzar *after* the Judeans had returned from exile and rebuilt their Temple (Judith 4:3; 5:18-19), but the Temple was only first destroyed and the Judeans exiled *after* Nebuchadnezzar's successful invasion. The story is also full of delicious irony from beginning to end, particularly in nearly everything Judith says to Holofernes (consider especially 11:5-6; 12:14, 18).

The story was probably composed in Hebrew in the land of Israel. It may well have been written in the decades following the Maccabean Revolt. The threat of the Temple's defilement (Judith 9:8) may reflect the more recent memory of the pollution of the Temple under Antiochus IV (see 1 Maccabees 1:41-50, 54; 2 Maccabees 6:1-7). Judith's manner of conquering the enemy and bringing safety to her people more closely resembles the diplomatic—and often deceptive—means by which Jonathan and Simon secured greater degrees of independence for Judea than the overt, military venues pursued while Judas was alive.

The Book of Judith is noteworthy for its openness to foreigners, even while speaking of Gentile hostility. Achior the Ammonite begins outside the covenant but is incorporated into Israel as the story progresses, since he essentially shares the Deuteronomistic view of Israel's history and the power of Israel's God to deliver God's people (see Judith 5:5–6:21; 14:6-10).

people of Canaan, whose land they will be invading, because God goes with them (Deuteronomy 20:1). This theme continues throughout the historical books of the Old Testament, where smaller Israelite armies defeat overwhelming foreign armies because God tips the scales (Judges 7:1-7; 1 Samuel 14:6; 1 Kings 18:19-37; also, 1 Maccabees 3:18-22) and reverberates also in the Psalms, where the worshipers declare their trust in God rather than in superior military strength (Psalm 20:7; see also 33:17-18). There are clearly some gender issues behind presenting a woman as the extreme example of what is weak, as opposed to military male power. God's bringing about the destruction of the enemy general, and thus enabling the routing of the invading army, "by the hand of a *woman*" (of all things!) magnifies God's power at the cost of maintaining certain cultural stereotypes of the woman as the weaker gender, less capable of acts of physical or military prowess than male soldiers (Judith 9:7-11; 16:5-6).

At the same time, however, the author of Judith calls these cultural stereotypes into question because, though physically weaker and more vulnerable, it is a woman who stands in the gap when the male elders falter in their commitment and conviction. The Book of Judith stands alongside texts like Fourth Maccabees, where a woman displays the utmost courage in the face of the storm of the emotions (4 Maccabees 14:11–17:6), proving the power of faith and training in God's Instruction to overcome any natural weaknesses. It stands alongside Plutarch's "On the Bravery of Women," a collection of episodes from Greek history in which women showed greater bravery than the men in their situations, accomplishing what the supposedly stronger sex ought to have done, but were too weak inwardly.

Holofernes has the strength of a vast army supplied by an economy of unlimited military spending, but he lacks control over himself. He is weak where it matters most. He does not examine the report of an emissary of the enemy, being too much taken with her beauty. He does not keep his wits about him as he brings this emissary into his bedroom with him alone, but abandons his guard to too much alcohol and sexual fantasies. His physical and military strength cannot compensate for his inner weakness. The male elders of the town of Bethulia cave in to the demands of the townspeople, rather than reminding them all of their duty to God and to the Temple in Jerusalem, which they must protect with their lives. They buy five more days of resistance to Holofernes, but agree to surrender when surrender is not a viable option in the larger scheme of things.

The woman Judith, together with her loyal servant, embodies courage and strength in this story. Her courage comes from an "all in" commitment to God, whether for life or death. Her courage allows her to walk into a camp full of military men after she has made herself look as stunning as possible when she knows how badly men at war can behave. Her courage allows her to stand before the most powerful general in the world and lie to his face, all the while maneuvering herself into a position to be alone with him. She uses all the skills at her disposal to play upon her enemy's weaknesses until, in a final act of courage, she holds a sword for the first time in her life and cuts off a person's head. She keeps her wits about her long enough to make a calm exit from the camp with her servant and return with her trophy to Bethulia, rallying her people to action the next morning.

The point of the story is not that God is so powerful that God can use *even* a woman. It's that a woman can be so courageous and committed to God that she can become an agent of God's deliverance. This role is not limited to males like Jonathan (in 1 Samuel 14:6) or Judas Maccabeus (in 1 Maccabees 3:18-22). The story is not without chauvinism, even as it challenges chauvinism.

There is a connection here with early Christian texts about women, which vacillate between a grand vision in which distinctions in gender (like ethnicity and social caste) have no value in God's sight and, therefore, no normative power for Christian community (Galatians 3:26-28) and more traditional statements about what is proper or improper for women (or "wives" vis-à-vis husbands; see 1 Corinthians 14:33-35; 1 Timothy 2:11-15). But we see something of Judith's courage in the women disciples who do not abandon Jesus during his passion and seek to care for his body after burial (Luke 23:27-31; 23:55–24:3), in Prisca, the more prominent member of the wife-and-husband apostolic team (Acts 18:24-28; Romans 16:3), in the female leaders within the early Christian movement (Romans 16:1-2; Philippians 4:2-3). We see her courage and commitment across the centuries, from the early martyrs Blandina, Perpetua, and Felicitas (see Eusebius, *Ecclesiastical History* 5.1.40-56; *Martyrdom of Perpetua and Felicitas*) to modern heroines Elisabeth Eliott, Asia Bibi, and Immaculee Ilibagiza. All such women of faith exhibit the strength that has value in God's sight and that positively advances God's purposes in this world.

The Problem With Bargaining With God

The people of Bethulia, to their credit, held out for a good while against impossible odds. Their water supply had been cut off, and they

Across the Testaments

Simeon and Levi: Good or Bad?

Readers of Judith may be surprised at her recollection of the story of Simeon and Levi's slaughter of the men of Shechem (Genesis 34). Judith says that God "put a sword into [Simeon's] hand to take revenge on the strangers who opened up a virgin's womb to pollute her," that God "handed over [Shechem's] rulers to be murdered" by God's "dearly loved children, who burned with holy zeal for you and hated the pollution of their blood" (Judith 9:2-4). The last word on Simeon and Levi in Genesis is Jacob's cursing of their anger and its violent results, passing over them to give the foremost blessing to Judah (Genesis 49:5-7).

While the author of Fourth Maccabees will retain this negative interpretation and judgment on Simeon and Levi (see 4 Maccabees 2:18-20), most intertestamental authors actually go in a strikingly different direction, overturning Jacob's verdict on the pair. A creative retelling of Genesis 1 through Exodus 14 known as *Jubilees*, written around 150 B.C. and authoritative for the community that produced the Dead Sea Scrolls, depicts Jacob agreeing with Simeon and Levi that revenge was required (though he took issue with the scope). The *Testament of Levi,* written at some point between 150 and 50 B.C., depicts Levi ascending in a vision to God's very throne, to receive a sword from God's hands to execute judgment on Shechem. He and Simeon chose to obey God rather than their father.

Such changes were probably motivated, in part, by the increasing interest in the boundaries between Jews and non-Jews. Levi and Simeon showed appropriate zeal for the purity of the people of Israel, much as Phinehas would later (see Numbers 25:6-13), for which Phinehas would be celebrated during this period (as in 1 Maccabees 2:23-26, 54; Sirach 45:23-25). The shift also reflects the veneration of Levi, in particular, as the ancestor of the priestly class. Indeed, in *Jubilees* and *Testament of Levi,* Levi receives the special honor of the priesthood as a result of his zeal and commitment to Israel's boundaries.

resisted surrender for thirty-four days until their water reserves were nearly exhausted. What, then, was so unreasonable about the elders' pact? They bought an extra five days of resistance against the enemy by making this deal with the townspeople. But surely they could not expect all the townspeople to willingly die of thirst!

Judith, however, takes them to task for striking this deal, for making a bargain with God, in effect. Either God will act in these next five days, or the people will abandon their post in their defense of God's Temple

(Judith 8:11). Such bargaining assumes that there are limits to devotion and commitment. Telling God to "do this by then, or else," assumes that there is some space after which human beings created by God no longer owe God and God's cause the same level of commitment, service, and obedience. Judith rejects this kind of thinking, arguing that God's people have only one course of action—to commit themselves to God's hands in loyal obedience to their duty toward God, whether this results in life or death (8:14b-16). Her stance closely resembles that of the three young men faced with the choice of disowning God by worshiping Nebuchadnezzar's idol or being thrown into a burning furnace: "If our God—the one we serve—is able to rescue us from the furnace of flaming fire and from your power, Your Majesty, then let him rescue us. But if he doesn't, know this for certain, Your Majesty: we will never serve your gods or worship the gold statue you've set up" (Daniel 3:17-18).

Equally important, however, is her cause for hope in this situation. Although Israel suffered devastation, conquest, and exile in the past, Judith believes that there is no reason to expect anything but help from God in the present time: "There hasn't been in our generation, nor is there today, a tribe, a family, a people, or a city among us who worships gods made with human hands as happened in times past. . . . Therefore, we hope that he won't forget about us and our generation" (Judith 8:18, 20). National security is again tied here to obedience to the covenant, the Instruction that God gave Moses. Earlier in Judith, Achior, commander of the Ammonite mercenaries who had offered their services to Holofernes, bore witness to the same conviction, though from *outside* the covenant (Judith 5:17, 20-21). Like the author of Second Maccabees, the author of Judith is firmly convinced that Deuteronomy 27–30 provides both a reliable lens for interpreting the past *and* looking ahead to the future. If the people keep faith with God by honoring the covenant and following its instructions, God will also surely keep faith with them.

It is probably not accidental that the author portrays the town as poised to give up after thirty-nine days (7:20, 30). Forty days is a well-known period of testing and living in the margins for God's sake. Noah and his family faced rain for this long (Genesis 7:12); Moses was on Mount

Sinai this long (Exodus 24:18; Deuteronomy 9:9); Elijah was in the desert en route to Horeb this long (1 Kings 19:8); Jesus would be tested in the desert this long (Mark 1:13). The elders and the townspeople were poised to fail their time of testing just one day short of that mark. Judith suggests that there is only one frame of mind to adopt if one wishes to pass the tests that come against one's faith: set no limits on how much you will endure out of fidelity to God, but be prepared to give all back to the one who gave all in the first place.

Live the Story

When was the last time you moved outside your comfort zone in response to God's call, or in response to meeting a clear need that God placed before you? Judith's story challenges us to dare more for the sake of God's purposes in our world, and her story assures us that God can indeed accomplish surprising things through the efforts of a faithful, committed individual who is willing to step forward. Paul would later affirm what Judith's story exemplifies: God's provision is sufficient, and God's power is most clearly shown in weak but willing, committed followers (see 2 Corinthians 4:1-7; 12:9-10).

What is too great for God to accomplish through you? Is it beyond God to establish a mentoring program for at-risk, inner-city youths through you? To mobilize support for families of persecuted Christians abroad and rally political leverage against the oppressive regimes? To create a network of churches that care for homeless families and help restore them to financial viability? To extend spiritual support and companionship to Christian sisters and brothers who have fallen afoul of the law and serve prison sentences?

Judith's story suggests to us that we see God at work too little in our world because we dare too little in God's name, with God's strength, and for God's sake. Her story—and Paul's theological legacy (see 1 Corinthians 1:18-31)—also suggests that God particularly delights in challenging the limitations that our cultural stereotypes seek to place upon us, and our own acceptance of living within those limits.

For Further Reading

Barclay, John M. G. *Jews in the Mediterranean Diaspora: from Alexander to Trajan (323 BCE–117 CE)*. Edinburgh: T. & T. Clark, 1996.

Beckwith, Roger T. *The Old Testament Canon of the New Testament Church: and its background in Early Judaism*. Grand Rapids: Eerdmans, 1985.

Bickerman, Elias J. *The Jews in the Greek Age*. Cambridge, MA: Harvard University Press, 1988.

Collins, John J. *Between Athens and Jerusalem: Jewish Identity in the Hellenistic Diaspora*. 2nd edition. Grand Rapids: Eerdmans, 2000.

deSilva, David A. *The Jewish Teachers of Jesus, James, and Jude: What Earliest Christianity Learned from the Apocrypha and Pseudepigrapha*. Oxford and New York: Oxford University Press, 2012.

_____. *The Apocrypha*. Core Biblical Studies. Nashville: Abingdon, 2012.

_____. *Introducing the Apocrypha: Message, Context, and Significance*. Grand Rapids: Baker Academic, 2002.

Dunn, James D. G., and John W. Rogerson (eds.). *Eerdmans Commentary on the Bible*. Grand Rapids: Wm. B. Eerdmans, 2003. Includes the Apocryphal/Deuterocanonical books.

Evans, Craig A. and Stanley E. Porter (eds.). *Dictionary of New Testament Background*. Downers Grove, IL: InterVarsity, 2002. Includes entries on each of the Apocryphal books and other Jewish texts from the period.

Harrington, Daniel J., S. J. *Invitation to the Apocrypha*. Grand Rapids: Eerdmans, 1999.

Kohlenberger III, John R. (ed.). *The Parallel Apocrypha*. New York: Oxford University, 1997.

Newsome, James D. *Greeks, Romans, Jews: Currents of Culture and Belief in the New Testament World*. Philadelphia: Trinity Press International, 1992.

Tcherikover, Victor. *Hellenistic Civilization and the Jews*. Philadelphia: Jewish Publication Society, 1959.

Voicu, Sever J. *Apocrypha*. Ancient Christian Commentary on Scripture. Downers Grove, Ill.: InterVarsity Press, 2010. A compendium of comments on most of the Apocryphal books by Christian teachers of the first eight centuries.

Leader Guide

People often view the Bible as a maze of obscure people, places, and events from centuries ago and struggle to relate it to their daily lives. IMMERSION invites us to experience the Bible as a record of God's loving revelation to humankind. These studies recognize our emotional, spiritual, and intellectual needs and welcome us into the Bible story and into deeper faith.

As leader of an IMMERSION group, you will help participants to encounter the Word of God and the God of the Word that will lead to new creation in Christ. You do not have to be an expert to lead; in fact, you will participate with your group in listening to and applying God's life-transforming Word to your lives. You and your group will explore the building blocks of the Christian faith through key stories, people, ideas, and teachings in every book of the Bible. You will also explore the bridges and points of connection between the Old and New Testaments.

Choosing and Using the Bible

The central goal of IMMERSION is engaging the members of your group with the Bible in a way that informs their minds, forms their hearts, and transforms the way they live out their Christian faith. Participants will need this study book and a Bible. IMMERSION is an excellent accompaniment to the Common English Bible (CEB). It shares with the CEB four common aims: clarity of language, faith in the Bible's power to transform lives, the emotional expectation that people will find the love of God, and the rational expectation that people will find the knowledge of God.

Other recommended study Bibles include *The New Interpreter's Study Bible* (NRSV), *The New Oxford Annotated Study Bible* (NRSV), *The HarperCollins Study Bible* (NRSV), the *NIV and TNIV Study Bibles*, and the *Archaeological Study Bible* (NIV). Encourage participants to use more than one translation. *The Message: The Bible in Contemporary Language* is a modern paraphrase of the Bible, based on the original languages. Eugene H. Peterson has created a masterful presentation of the Scripture text, which is best used alongside rather than in place of the CEB or another primary English translation.

One of the most reliable interpreters of the Bible's meaning is the Bible itself. Invite participants first of all to allow Scripture to have its say. Pay attention to context. Ask questions of the text. Read every passage with curiosity, always seeking to answer the basic Who? What? Where? When? and Why? questions.

Bible study groups should also have handy essential reference resources in case someone wants more information or needs clarification on specific words, terms, concepts, places, or people mentioned in the Bible. A Bible dictionary, Bible atlas, concordance, and one-volume Bible commentary together make for a good, basic reference library.

The Leader's Role

An effective leader prepares ahead. This leader guide provides easy-to-follow, step-by-step suggestions for leading a group. The key task of the leader is to guide discussion and activities that will engage heart and head and will invite faith development. Discussion questions are included, and you may want to add questions posed by you or your group. Here are suggestions for helping your group engage Scripture:

State questions clearly and simply.

Ask questions that move Bible truths from "outside" (dealing with concepts, ideas, or information about a passage) to "inside" (relating to the experiences, hopes, and dreams of the participants).

Work for variety in your questions, including compare and contrast, information recall, motivation, connections, speculation, and evaluation.

Avoid questions that call for yes-or-no responses or answers that are obvious.

Don't be afraid of silence during a discussion. It often yields especially thoughtful comments.

Test questions before using them by attempting to answer them yourself.

When leading a discussion, pay attention to the mood of your group by "listening" with your eyes as well as your ears.

Guidelines for the Group

IMMERSION is designed to promote full engagement with the Bible for the purpose of growing faith and building up Christian community. While much can be gained from individual reading, a group Bible study offers an ideal setting in which to achieve these aims. Encourage participants to bring their Bibles and read from Scripture during the session. Invite participants to consider the following guidelines as they participate in the group:

Respect differences of interpretation and understanding.

Support one another with Christian kindness, compassion, and courtesy.

Listen to others with the goal of understanding rather than agreeing or disagreeing.

Celebrate the opportunity to grow in faith through Bible study.

Approach the Bible as a dialogue partner, open to the possibility of being challenged or changed by God's Word.

Recognize that each person brings unique and valuable life experiences to the group and is an important part of the community.

Reflect theologically—that is, be attentive to three basic questions: What does this say about God? What does this say about me/us? What does this say about the relationship between God and me/us?

Commit to a lived faith response in light of insights you gain from the Bible. In other words, what changes in attitudes (how you believe) or actions (how you behave) are called for by God's Word?

Group Sessions

The group sessions, like the chapters themselves, are built around three sections: "Claim Your Story," "Enter the Bible Story," and "Live the Story." Sessions are designed to move participants from an awareness of their own life story, issues, needs, and experiences into an encounter and dialogue with the story of Scripture and to make decisions integrating their personal stories and the Bible's story.

The session plans in the following pages will provide questions and activities to help your group focus on the particular content of each chapter. In addition to questions and activities, the plans will include chapter title, Scripture, and faith focus.

Here are things to keep in mind for all the sessions:

Prepare Ahead

Study the Scripture, comparing different translations and perhaps a paraphrase.

Read the chapter, and consider what it says about your life and the Scripture.

Gather materials such as large sheets of paper or a markerboard with markers.

Prepare the learning area. Write the faith focus for all to see.

Welcome Participants

Invite participants to greet one another.

Tell them to find one or two people and talk about the faith focus.

Ask: What words stand out for you? Why?

Guide the Session

Look together at "Claim Your Story." Ask participants to give their reactions to the stories and examples given in each chapter. Use questions from the session plan to elicit comments based on personal experiences and insights.

Ask participants to open their Bibles and "Enter the Bible Story." For each portion of Scripture, use questions from the session plan to help participants gain insight into the text and relate it to issues in their own lives.

Step through the activity or questions posed in "Live the Story." Encourage participants to embrace what they have learned and to apply it in their daily lives.

Invite participants to offer their responses or insights about the boxed material in "Across the Testaments," "About the Scripture," and "About the Christian Faith."

Close the Session

Encourage participants to read the following week's Scripture and chapter before the next session.

Offer a closing prayer.

1. What Is the Apocrypha, and Why Should We Care?
Apocrypha

Faith Focus

A collection of inspirational books loved and used by early Christians can evoke faithful responses to God in twenty-first-century Christians and a seeking after God's will and favor.

Before the Session

1. Look up the words *apocrypha* and *canon.* Write the definitions on a large sheet of paper, a posterboard, or a markerboard.

2. List the following words and names on posterboard, a large piece of paper, or a markerboard: "Tobit," "Judith," "Esther," "Solomon," "Sirach," "Baruch," "Jeremiah," "Daniel," "Maccabees," "Esdras," "Manasseh," "Susannah," "Bel and the Snake," "Exodus," "Jerusalem," "Palestine," "Judea," "Egypt," "Psalms," "Samuel," "Goliath," "Herod."

3. Be prepared to show a map of the Mediterranean area, large enough that everyone can see.

Claim Your Story

Dr. deSilva explains that the Apocrypha has often been shunned by Bible scholars and students in recent times. Ask the group for a show of hands from those who have ever read any part of the Apocrypha. Ask the group to tell about their own experiences with the Apocrypha. Have they been warned about reading it? Do they have negative feelings? How do they feel now about beginning a study of the Apocrypha? Are they excited? wary?

Enter the Bible Story

Remind the group that the dates for writing of the Apocrypha begin about 250 B.C. and end about A.D. 100. Explain that this would have covered a couple of centuries just prior to Jesus' birth, all the years of Jesus life, and the period just after Jesus death and resurrection. These stories would have been familiar to Jesus. They would be stories told in his home.

Show the list of names and words you have prepared. These all come from the Apocrypha. As you read a name or word, ask the group to hold up their hands if they have ever heard it before. Mark next to each name or word on the list how many know and don't know it. Many will be unknown by the group, but many will be familiar to everyone. Explain that all are from the books of the Apocrypha. Even if they have not read any of these stories, they will already be familiar enough to feel comfortable.

Ask why Israel/Palestine was so important in biblical times. Show the map and ask someone to point to Rome, Egypt, Syria, and the countries east of Syria. Now point out Israel and tell everyone that Israel/Palestine was in the middle of all the political/cultural/religious conflict. This is the background of the life Jesus lived.

The lesson writer said that in the midst of this political-cultural-religious milieu a "major challenge had to do with the choice between assimilation and remaining 'holy to the Lord.' " Can the group find any similarities with their own rapidly changing pluralistic society? Does it present temptations to mix in and mix up their faith? What is appropriate in assimilation? As Hellenism made a "positive contribution to the repertoire of Jewish wisdom and self-understanding," how can modern cultures contribute to our own?

Turn the discussion to the collection and use of the books of the Apocrypha.

Ask the group for definitions of *apocrypha* and *canon*. Then share the definitions you found in the dictionary.

Dr. deSilva wrote that there were many books available to read during the first century A.D. There were variations of some books of the Scripture, like Daniel and Esther. There were many gospels besides the four in our Bible. And letters were being written, read, and studied. Ask the group how the New Testament could ever have been written if only the Hebrew Scriptures were studied. Ask the group whether their favorite Bible contains the Apocrypha.

Ask the group to review the points of Martin Luther's position on the Apocrypha and to discuss the merits of Luther's argument. Do they agree or disagree?

Live the Story

Do group members agree that "the golden age of divine inspiration is behind us"? Do they read spiritual and devotional books today? Who are some of their favorite writers? Do they feel their favorites are inspired?

Ask the group if they have family members or friends who are models they hold up for inspiration?

Have group members ever felt God was talking directly to them? Lead the group in a prayer for God to be present in their lives every hour, every day.

Leave five minutes at the end of the session to ask if there were any points in the lesson that need discussion and clarification. Discuss. Suggest that remaining questions could be contemplated during the week and cleared up at the beginning of the next session.

2. Tobit
Tobit 1–14

Faith Focus
Life sometimes comes to times and places where despair sets in and there seems to be no way forward. Just then God changes everything for the better with the gift of generous kindness.

Before the Session
Look up the words *despair, patience,* and *persistence.* Write the words and definitions on posterboard or a large sheet of paper.

Prepare some strips of paper by cutting 8 1/2 x 11 sheets of paper into two-inch strips. Have a strip and a pencil or pen for every person.

Claim Your Story
Dr. deSilva leads our minds to times of despair, when we pray, "God, just end my misery." Ask group members to volunteer a story from their own lives.

The lesson suggests that there is truth in the saying that bad things happen to good people. Do members of the group feel their commitment to doing what is right doesn't seem to pay off? Do we have an agreement with God to receive blessings for doing what is right?

Enter the Bible Story
Tobit and his family are described in the lesson as "just good church folk." In the Broadway show *Camelot,* King Arthur and Guinevere sing, "What do the simple folk do to help them escape when they're blue?" Does God ever need to ask about the simple folk? Or is staying in touch with our needs something only we humans have difficulty managing?

Tobit has lost the ability to believe that good things happen and is shocked by Anna's employer's generosity. Sarah despairs of ever having a family after seven wedding night dead grooms. Both Tobit and Sarah have prayed consistently to God without a satisfying answer. So both change their prayers to petitions for God to end their miserable lives.

Display the words and definitions you have written. Ask group members: When is despair reached? What does it look like in real-life situations? Where is the end of persistence? How much patience is enough patience? How does all of this relate to faith and prayer?

Tobit is held up as a model for charitable giving. God's appreciation and reward can be expected. "Giving assistance to the poor rescues a person from death and keeps a person from going down into darkness" (Tobit 4:10). Is being a "checkbook" Christian good enough?

Call attention to the grid that compares Tobit and the teachings of Jesus on page 28. Choose one or two comparisons and have someone read the verses from Tobit and another read the corresponding passage in the Gospel. Then ask the group to tell of someone whom they know who models this same generosity.

Marriage is a major theme in the Book of Tobit. Ask someone to read Genesis 2:21-24 and another person to read Tobit 8:5-8. Ask group members to compare the two readings. Follow-up with asking about the importance of good relations between in-laws.

While nothing seemed to be going right for Tobias and Sarah in their separate, distant lives, God seems to have had a plan for them. Eventually, they are brought together and life is truly wonderful thereafter. Ask the group members if they have ever had the experience of knowing great frustration or pain and then many years later looking back and being able to see God's good plan for them. Ask them to share their personal story. Now make the discussion more difficult. Why did all of Sarah's husbands die? What collateral damage (sometimes associated with good) do we all experience in life. Why?

Dr. deSilva explains that the quantity of discovered books suggests the importance of the book and the love people have for them. Ask the group to name best-selling books that suggest what is culturally or religiously important to American people today.

Live the Story

Hand out the paper strips and pencils to everyone and ask them to write one thing they will do this week to be generous to others. Then ask them to turn the paper over and write a need for persistent prayer. Ask them to hold the paper against their heart and then pray this prayer:

> Dear Loving God,
> As you are generous, let me be generous. As you are persistent, let me be persistent. Let me always stay close to you. Amen.

Instruct the group members to place their slip of paper in their Bible.

Leave five minutes at the end of the session to ask if there were any points in the lesson that need discussion and clarification. Discuss. Suggest that remaining questions could be contemplated during the week and cleared up at the beginning of the next session.

3. Second Maccabees
2 Maccabees 2:19–10:38

Faith Focus
God, with great love, offers a covenant to humankind. There are real consequences for keeping or breaking the covenant. The best course of action is always to choose faithfulness to the covenant.

Before the Session
Look in the dictionary for the definition of *covenant* and write it on posterboard or a large sheet of paper.

Write on posterboard, a markerboard, or a large sheet of paper the following Scripture references:

- Covenant with Adam: Genesis 2:16-17
- Covenant with Noah: Genesis 9:9-17
- Covenant with Abraham: Genesis 15:8-18; 17:9-14
- Covenant with Moses: Exodus 24:4-8
- Covenant with David: Psalm 89:3-4
- New Covenant: John 1:12-13; Romans 10:9-10; Hebrews 8:6-13

Find a liturgy for reaffirmation of baptism for your denomination and prepare to read it to the group.

Claim Your Story
Say to the group, "If you will follow in your lesson book, listen to my instructions, and read in your Bible, I will help you learn about the Maccabees and *covenant*." Ask everyone in the group if they agree. When they agree, say, "Fine. We have just made a covenant."

Ask the group to name covenants they have made recently and how determined they are to remain in the covenant.

Enter the Bible Story
Ask the group to open their Bibles to Deuteronomy 28:1-14. Have them call out the many blessings God promises and list them on posterboard, markerboard, or a large sheet of paper. How many did they list? Now count the number of times the covenant speaks of obedience to God's commands. How is the covenant balanced?

Reveal the definition of the word *covenant* that you have copied onto paper. Now show the list of covenant Scripture references. Have individuals or partners read as many aloud as time allows. Encourage everyone to write down the references so they can look them up after the group meets.

Second Maccabees is both a story of a heroic family and the nation of Israel. It is a familiar story for Israel. Under the high priest Onias III the people remain faithful to their covenant with God and they prosper. When Jason becomes high priest, he rejects their responsibility in the covenant and their fortunes decline. Some argue today that our nation suffers many ills because we are not faithful to our Judeo/Christian ordinances. What are some of the arguments? How convincing are they?

Venerable Eleazar and the mother with seven sons were forced to eat pork against their Jewish law. Eleazer refused (he even refused to trick the officials lest young Jews think he accepted the pork). All accepted martyrdom and experienced gruesome deaths. For what might group members be willing to be martyred? How much humiliation and pain could they endure to stand for what they believe? Is it possible to know that we would stand firm, should we be challenged? Would they try to accommodate in some way?

The Hebrews of Second Maccabees had a firm belief in resurrection from the dead. Point out that this is a good bridge story to Jesus the Savior, his martyrdom, resurrection, and ascension. Does knowing that death is not the final answer and you will be raised from the dead make it easier to consider martyrdom?

Return to the theme of the importance of the apocryphal books to the early Christians by reviewing "About the Christian Faith" on page 37. Consider especially that the Maccabean martyrs were the only non-Christian Jews to be counted among the saints of the church.

Live the Story

Early in the lesson we learned that the Hebrews of the Book of Deuteronomy were mostly second- and third-generation exiles from Egypt. They were not original parties to the covenant. How many of us are Christians (and members of our denomination) because of our parents and grandparents? Many of us were baptized as infants, with the commitment of our parents. How firmly attached to a covenant with God are we? Attached firmly enough to defend it with our lives?

Lead group members in writing a new covenant to God the Father, with the Son, and the Holy Spirit.

Share this reaffirmation of the Baptismal Covenant with the group:

Reaffirmation of the Baptismal Covenant

Through the Sacrament of Baptism
  we are initiated into Christ's holy church.
We are incorporated into God's mighty acts of salvation
  and given new birth through water and the Spirit.
All this is God's gift, offered to us without price.

Through the reaffirmation of our faith
we renew the covenant declared at our baptism,
  acknowledge what God is doing for us,
  and affirm our commitment to Christ's holy church.[1]

Leave five minutes at the end of the session to ask if there were any points in the lesson that need discussion and clarification. Discuss. Suggest that remaining questions could be contemplated during the week and cleared up at the beginning of the next session.

1. *The United Methodist Hymnal* (Nashville: The United Methodist Publishing House, 1989), 50.

4. Fourth Maccabees
4 Maccabees 1–7; Galatians 5–6

Faith Focus
By loving God and learning and practicing spiritual disciplines we can defeat the power of our selfish desires and passions.

Before the Session
Look up the definitions for the words *passions* and *desires*. Write them on posterboard or a large sheet of paper.

Write on a large sheet of paper or posterboard Richard Foster's list of spiritual disciplines (from his book *Celebration of Discipline*; HarperSanFrancisco, 2002). (You might prepare this as a handout for group members to take home with them.)

1. The inward disciplines: meditation, prayer, fasting, study
2. The outward disciplines (inward realities resulting in outward lifestyles): simplicity, solitude, submission, service
3. The corporate disciplines: confession, worship, guidance, celebration

Assemble an empty clear bottle, some large stones that will fit into the bottle, some smaller pebbles, and some sand. Keep all of these items separate until you assemble them during the lesson.

Claim Your Story
Ask group members what talents they have for which they have developed special skills. How long did it take them to develop the skills? What training routines did they practice? Did they practice and develop these skills because they wanted to or because someone pushed them? How important was encouragement from someone else?

Enter the Bible Story
The lesson lists greed, lust, envy, and anger as emotions against which we should fight. What are some others? How are these harmful? To whom are these emotions harmful?

Show the definitions for *passions* and *desires* that you have previously prepared. How do these emotions fit the definitions? Ask the group members how successful they have been in allowing God into their lives to overcome the emotions they have just discussed. What sorts of problems have they encountered in attempting to resist the passions and desires?

Now ask, What training have you had in your life that did (or can) help you resist? What was the role of parents? teachers? mentors? Sunday school teachers? pastors? friends? the Bible? Ask if group members have "trained" for morality in the same way that they trained for the skills they told about earlier in the discussion.

Dr. deSilva writes that "God has sent a personal Trainer to work alongside us, to put us through the appropriate paces, to encourage us, even to empower us on the road to moral transformation. . . ." Ask someone to read Galatians 5:22-23. Now lead people to the grid on pages 44-45. Divide the participants into two- or three-person small groups and assign to each a reading in Maccabees and its parallel Old Testament reading. Ask each group to discuss how the practical regulations found in the Scriptures help to "train" a person for good moral living. How do they relate to Galatians 5:22-23?

Live the Story

Show Richard Foster's list of spiritual disciplines. Ask the group members to select some discipline from each of the three groups and commit to working on that discipline during the week. Ask them to evaluate their effort at the end of the week.

Take the bottle, stones, pebbles, and sand you have prepared ahead of time and show them to the group. Say, "Life is like this bottle. You can fill it with anything you like. You can choose good or bad. If your bottle is filled with bad, you can change it." Place larger stones in the bottle. Say, "Replace some of the bad with the stones of virtue. Do you want to remove more of the bad? Add some pebbles of goodness." Add the small pebbles to the bottle so that they fill space around the larger stones. Say, "Want to rid yourself of bad? Add the sand of holiness." Pour sand in the bottle until all the empty space is filled. Hold the bottle higher and say, "See, there is now no room for the bad emotions and desires you formerly had."

Leave five minutes at the end of the session to ask if there were any points in the lesson that need discussion and clarification. Discuss. Suggest that remaining questions could be contemplated during the week and cleared up at the beginning of the next session.

Close with prayer.

5. Prayers of Repentance in the Apocrypha
Prayer of Manasseh; Prayer of Azariah; Baruch 1:1–3:8

Faith Focus
By examining our own behavior and repenting of our wrongdoing, Christians can defeat anger and bitterness and strengthen their relationship with a just and merciful God.

Before the Session
Look up the definitions of the words *confession, repentance, justice,* and *mercy.* Write them on posterboard or a large sheet of paper.

Research Dietrich Bonhoeffer on the Internet and be prepared to briefly tell about his resistance to the Nazis in World War II.

Have a large sheet of paper or posterboard available to write on when the group composes a prayer at the end of the session.

Claim Your Story
Dr. deSilva writes about serious anger with God and even claims occasional feelings that God fails us. Ask the group members to tell stories of times they felt disappointment and anger with God.

Enter the Bible Story
The lesson gives the story of three Bible characters and the terrible events that came to them. What were the similarities and differences between Baruch, Manasseh, and Azariah?

Display the definitions of *confession, repentance, justice,* and *mercy.* Ask the group to identify all four concepts in the stories of the three men.

Ask three persons to read the three passages from the Apocrypha that are printed on page 53. Ask group members how easy it is to accept responsibility for their misdeeds. What roles do obstinance, fear, and regret play in confession? Are there other emotions that come into play? What would justice look like if we didn't have God's grace?

Baruch, Manasseh, and Azariah all suggest that there is some sort of communal responsibility even when we are not personally liable for wrongdoing. Dr. deSilva writes that "if the problem is with our people, we have prophetic witness and confrontation" in our repertoire of responses. Ask: When we believe that our church or community is going in the wrong direction, what is our responsibility as a church member or community citizen?

Manasseh was a truly wicked man. Every age has its truly wicked people. Manasseh searched himself and asked God for forgiveness and mercy. God's anger was so great that even good King Josiah could not make up for Manasseh. Discuss how bystanders and innocent people suffer because of others' misdeeds. Who suffers during war? How is this fair or just? Who are some of the persons who have done great harm to others in the lifetime of group members? Are there signs of repentance among any of them? Is it fair or just for an evil person to receive mercy after harming others? Do you agree with Dr. deSilva that "no individual [is] beyond repentance and reconciliation"?

Tell the story of Dietrich Bonhoeffer and his resistance to the Nazis. He sacrificed his life for his Christian principles. Ask the group to discuss this story and make comparison to the stories of Baruch and Azariah.

Ask someone to read the portion of prayers from Azariah 11 and from Baruch 2 printed on page 58. Lead group members in a discussion of the importance of maintaining God's reputation and honor. Ask why this is important. How do we magnify the Lord and hallow the Lord's name?

Live the Story

Often the passage of time allows for a new perspective on serious and painful circumstances or events. How have members changed their attitudes about some of the disappointments and anger that they told in the opening of the "Claim Your Story" part of the discussion? What resolutions did they find and how did they come about?

The beautiful line in Prayer of Manasseh, "Now I bend the knee of my heart, begging you to show kindness," can be an inspiration and a starting point for group members to write prayers. Divide the participants into three groups. Instruct one group to write a prayer of personal self-examination, confession, and repentance. Instruct the second group to write a prayer of community self-examination, confession, and repentance. Ask the third group to write a prayer magnifying God for the gifts of grace and mercy. End the group session by reading the prayers aloud.

Leave five minutes at the end of the session to ask if there were any points in the lesson that need discussion and clarification. Discuss. Suggest that remaining questions could be contemplated during the week and cleared up at the beginning of the next session.

6. Sirach
Sirach selections

Faith Focus
God's people revere wisdom and seek it. Their standard for true wisdom is alignment with God's will and commands.

Before the Session
Write the Faith Focus statement on a large sheet of paper or on poster-board.

Research online the concept of small-scale loans begun with an economics professor named Muhammad Yunus who started the Grameen Bank in 1979 after arguing that the 50 percent of Bangladeshis who are landless and the 80 percent who are illiterate could still be good credit risks.

Assemble photos of people, landscapes, and things that most people would find awe-inspiring.

Have copies of Sunday's worship bulletin to distribute to the group members.

Keep blank sheets of paper or posterboard handy for use in the group meeting.

Claim Your Story
Much of what we consider our personal wisdom came to us a long time ago, in our early years. There are some things we seemed to have known all our life. Ask group members to close their eyes and think back to when they were small children. Ask them to remember some lesson they learned long ago and have held on to ever since. What was that lesson? What was the circumstance? Who taught the lesson? Was it a painful or joyous lesson at the time? How has it served them through the years?

Enter the Bible Story
Ask someone to read Sirach 1:28 and 2:12. Ask someone else to read James 4:4. Then read the following famous words of Abraham Lincoln:

"A house divided against itself cannot stand. I believe this government cannot endure, permanently, half slave and half free. I do not expect the Union to be dissolved—I do not expect the house to fall—but I do expect it will cease to be divided. It will become all one thing or all the other."

We all know that slavery was abolished in the United States. Ask the group members to discuss the readings from Sirach and James and the speech of Abraham Lincoln in light of this lesson's Faith Focus statement, which you can now display. Ask: Can your selfish will stand against what you know to be right and where you think God is leading you? Discuss how you work through conflicting courses of action in your life.

Wisdom is nothing if it is not put to good use. And wisdom does not reside only in selected life aspects. Ask half the group members to turn in their Bibles to any chapter of Sirach. Ask the other half to turn in their Bibles to any chapter of Proverbs. Have everyone scan the texts to find sayings that appeal to them and ask one person to read from Sirach, then one person to read from Proverbs until all have shared a saying.

Then on a large sheet of paper or on posterboard, write of list of the topics covered in the two books.

Ask someone to read aloud Sirach 29:8-13. Share what you learned in researching Muhammed Yunus and his Grameen Bank in Bangladesh. Ask: How does his very practical advice and his enormous success parallel that of Ben Sira and our Faith Focus statement today?

Display the pictures of awe-inspiring people, places, and things that you have collected. Ask the group to tell what inspires them to think of God's greatness.

Distribute the worship bulletins and ask group members what part(s) of the worship service mean the most to them and why. What part of the liturgy means the least to them? Why? What changes would help them truly worship their great God?

Direct group members to the grid on pages 67-68. In as much time as you have, request group members read aloud paired passages from Sirach and the New Testament and then discuss the wisdom concept presented by both.

Live the Story

Ask each group member to recall the life lesson they remembered and shared during the Claim Your Story section of the discussion. After studying wisdom does their life lesson measure up to the standard of godliness?

Tell or read the following story:

"A Christian man lived far away from his beloved alcoholic and homeless brother. Many hospitalizations and counseling sessions paid for by the caring brother had failed. Every month the man looked for an occasion to send something good to his brother: warm clothing during the winter months, nonperishable food for his birthday, allergy medicine when he knew it was needed. A case worker told him he was wasting his money because the troubled brother sold all that was sent and used the money to buy alcohol."

Ask the group what godly wisdom would direct the good man to do upon hearing what happened to his gifts. Why?

Leave five minutes at the end of the session to ask if there were any points in the lesson that need discussion and clarification. Discuss. Suggest that remaining questions could be contemplated during the week and cleared up at the beginning of the next session.

Close the session with prayer for godly wisdom.

7. Wisdom of Solomon
Wisdom 1–5

Faith Focus
People of faith understand that they can do nothing greater than to live the lifespan given to them doing what is good according to their Creator God.

Before the Session
Look up the word *virtue* and print the definition on a large sheet of paper or on posterboard.

Have paper and pencils ready to distribute to everyone.

Claim Your Story
Before beginning any lecture or conversation, distribute paper and pencils to everyone and announce, "You have been named in a secret benefactor's will. Five hundred thousand dollars has been given to you to use as you like. Take your paper and pencil and make a list of ways you will use the money. Number the items on your list according to priority."

Now, read or retell Claim Your Story. Ask the group members to review their list of spending priorities. Would they like to share their lists with the group? What does their list say about their values? Do their lists show a selfish or a generous person? Remind group members that they had not earned the inheritance, that someone had given it to them in complete selflessness.

Enter the Bible Story
Ask the group to take the paper they used earlier and turn it over to make a list of all the things they would like to do if they no longer had to work. They have all the time and other resources to do whatever they please. After they have completed the list, ask them how many items refer to their own pleasures and desires and how many refer to the welfare or enjoyment of others? What is their "me/others" quotient? Have them turn to the person sitting next to them and discuss how well balanced their list is.

Point out that Dr. deSilva says, "Our perception of death can distort our lives." If we think that death is absolutely the end, we may well believe that we should acquire and use as much as we can in life. That's all there is. Period.

On the other hand, Dr. deSilva speaks of a different choice. Ask the group what that other way is. The answer is a *grasp of God's purpose for our lives.* Dr. deSilva says this makes us "more humane and humble in the face of our shared mortality."

Display the definition of the word *virtue* and point out that Dr. deSilva says that "virtue . . . often takes its starting point from measuring the value and needs of the other [person]. . . ." Ask group members to name persons, famous or otherwise, living or dead, who fit the dictionary definition of virtue and Dr. deSilva's starting point for virtue. Describe their conduct that earns a place for them on a list of virtuous people.

Ask someone to read aloud Genesis 1:27 and Genesis 2:15. In fact, humans, being made in the image of God, share God's immortality. Ask someone to read Wisdom 2:23–3:5. Ask: What is the role of grasping God's purpose for our lives? How do these readings from Genesis and Wisdom of Solomon affirm that?

Ask someone to read aloud Proverbs 8:22-31 and someone else to read aloud Wisdom 7:22-26. Wisdom is portrayed as a woman, a woman sent from God to earth. Ask: How does this lead into the story of God sending his Son to earth? Refer to Dr. deSilva's discussion of Wisdom and God in the formulation of the relationship of God and the Son in the Nicene Creed.

Ask someone to read aloud Wisdom 13:6-9 and some else to read aloud John 1:9-14. Ask the group to make comparisons and contrasts between the two passages. Ask how John ends differently than Wisdom.

Live the Story

Ask the group members to look again at the two lists they made earlier in the session. Instruct them to edit their sheets any way they please in light of the day's lessons.

Leave five minutes at the end of the session to ask if there were any points in the lesson that need discussion and clarification. Discuss. Suggest that remaining questions could be contemplated during the week and cleared up at the beginning of the next session.

End the group session with a prayer that asks God for wisdom and for commitment to live a life in accordance with God's purpose.

8. Judith
Judith 8–16

Faith Focus
People of God believe, even in the worst of times, that God's promises to them will be fulfilled, and they will do everything in their power in order to fulfill their commitment to God.

Before the Session
On the Internet look up early Christian women "Blandina," "Perpetua," and "Felicitas." Also look up modern Christian women "Elizabeth Elliot," "Asia Bibi," and "Immaculee Ilibagiza." Be prepared to tell a little bit about each woman's story and what makes each notable.

Fold a large piece of paper in half. Fold it a second time in half so that it is now quartered. Leave folded to use as an exhibit later. One corner of the folded paper is the actual fold at the center of the paper. When instructed during the Live Your Story section, you will tear off about an inch of this corner.

Claim Your Story
Read aloud the first half of Claim Your Story ending with the question, "What can God do about it though me?" Ask: Who did anything for you in this past week that made you feel just a little bit better? Who improved your life in some small way? What did that person do? And how did it help you? After discussion ask, Can we say that these people changed your world?

Enter the Bible Story
Judith was a remarkable woman in all respects. Among other things, this book in the Apocrypha is a tribute to strong women. Hold up the names of Elizabeth Elliot, who served God in Ecuador with her husband Jim and survived his execution in 1956; Asia Bibi, who is currently jailed in Pakistan for refusing to give up her Christian faith; and Immaculee Ilibagiza, who lost most of her family in the 1994 Rwandan genocide, yet continues to tell all the world about the holiness and mercy of God.

Ask: How are these modern women demonstrating strength of character and faith to the world?

Say, "These women exhibit extraordinary courage in exceptional circumstances. Who are some women you know in your family or community, who are perhaps not heroic, but who exhibit courage and faith that inspires you?"

General Holofernes is told that the Jews are special and have a God who protects his people as long as they are faithful to the covenant God has made with them. Story after story in the Bible shows this to be true. Ask: Since we are God's people, can we expect this to be true for us?

There are people in our country today who, in the name of Jesus Christ, claim that our country is not upholding the covenant with God and that is the reason we have natural calamities and have wars and other human-caused tragedies. Ask: Do you believe we are still under God's protection?

Judith was an "all or nothing" follower of God. When the Bethulia leaders bargained with Holofernes, she was enraged that they did not give all their trust to God that God would protect them. When she went to Holofernes's camp she lied, seductively played on her sexuality, and murdered. All this for God? Ask: Are there limits in our relationship with God? If yes, how do we define them?

Some Christians believe that complete compliance with God's commands means that when injured or ill, they cannot go to a doctor nor receive a blood transfusion. Ask: Do you suppose Judith would agree with these people? Do you agree? Why?

The leaders of Bethulia set a date when they would stop expecting God's rescue and when they would give up the town to Holofernes. Ask: How long is too long to wait for God's action?

Live the Story

Ask: Who in this group has the courage to change the world? After there are answers or no answers, ask: What does it mean to change the world? What will it take?

After some discussion, hold up the piece of paper that you have folded in quarters. Say, "This piece of paper represents the world. It is folded in quarters to represent the proverbial four corners of the earth. We think we have neither the brains, resources, power, nor courage to step out and change the world. But let me show you something. I am tearing off this folded corner of the world to represent the changes you and I can make. It seems very small. But when I open the paper so that you can see all four corners of the world, look! Because I have made one small change, all the world is affected. We do have the power to change the world!"

Ask: Now what can we do in our small place to change the world? After discussion, end the session in prayer, asking God for the means to help God change the world.

Leave five minutes at the end of the session to ask if there were any points in the lesson that need discussion and clarification. Discuss.

Close with prayer.

IMMERSE YOURSELF IN ANOTHER VOLUME
IMMERSION
Bible Studies

Genesis	9781426716232
Exodus, Leviticus, Numbers	9781426716324
Deuteronomy	9781426716331
Joshua, Judges, Ruth	9781426716348
1 & 2 Samuel, 1 & 2 Kings, 1 & 2 Chronicles	9781426716355
Ezra, Nehemiah, Esther	9781426716362
Job	9781426716300
Psalms	9781426716294
Proverbs, Ecclesiastes, Song of Solomon	9781426716317
Isaiah, Jeremiah, Lamentations	9781426716379
Ezekiel, Daniel	9781426716386
Hosea, Joel, Amos, Obadiah, Jonah	9781426716393
Micah, Nahum, Habakkuk, Zephaniah, Haggai, Zechariah, Malachi	9781426716409
Apocrypha	9781426742972
Matthew	9781426709821
Mark	9781426709166
Luke	9781426709838
John	9781426709845
Acts	9781426709852
Romans	9781426709869
1 & 2 Corinthians	9781426709876
Galatians, Ephesians, Philippians	9781426710841
Colossians, 1 & 2 Thessalonians	9781426710858
1 & 2 Timothy, Titus, Philemon	9781426709906
Hebrews	9781426709890
James; 1 & 2 Peter; 1, 2 & 3 John; Jude	9781426709883
Revelation	9781426709920

Available at Cokesbury and other booksellers   AbingdonPress.com

BKM126600001 PACP01238834-01